W9-BKT-908

HD
1379
.S65x

Speraw, Linda

How to buy your first
home

DATE DUE			
JAN 25 '84	OCT 09 1996		
OCT 2 '85	DEC 02 1996		
NOV 14 '86	APR 04 2006		
NOV 02 1987			
NOV 24 1988			
AUG 01 1989			
SEP 03 1990			
MAY 30 '91			
JUL 08 '91			
JUL 27 1993			
MAR 14 1995			

HOW TO BUY
YOUR FIRST
HOME

HOW TO BUY
YOUR FIRST
HOME

Linda Speraw

Facts On File Publications
460 Park Avenue South
New York, N.Y. 10016

HOW TO BUY YOUR FIRST HOME

Library of Congress Cataloging in Publication Data

Speraw, Linda.
    How to buy your first house.

    Includes index.
    1. House buying. 2. Housing—Finance.
3. Mortgages. I. Title.
HD1379.S65   643'.12   81-19559
ISBN 0-87196-609-3   AACR2

Printed in the United States of America

10 9 8 7 6 5 4 3 2 1

CONTENTS

PREFACE

Owning a home is synonymous with "the American dream." A home offers shelter, security, possibly a yard for the kids, a place to plug in the washer and dryer, a garage for the table saw, a yard for the dog, a spot for the avocado tree that you now have growing in a jar in the kitchen window, a fireplace . . . room for expansion. Buying a home provides pride of ownership today, and represents an investment in tomorrow.

Acquiring real estate is not a *venture*. Real estate is the most solid, high-return investment available. Why? Because everyone needs it. But today surging inflation and high interest are making ownership of real estate, especially prime urban and suburban properties, inaccessible to all but the rich. Americans are facing a major dilemma. The "we can't afford to buy a house" syndrome is counter-balanced only by cultural conditioning that leads us to believe anything is possible once our minds are put to it. This is the *only* attitude for today's prospective homebuyers, because you can still buy. *There is always someone out there who needs to sell; to somebody's problem, you represent the solution.*

The need to sell real estate can arise for any number of

reasons. Someone has inherited property they don't want to bother managing. A lucrative new job may require relocation and a fast sell. A couple is retiring and moving to the country. And the financial position of these people who are selling their homes may help you achieve what you want. Are these sellers wealthy people who want to avoid excessive taxes? Are they about to retire—and, if so, would they prefer to have a monthly income rather than receiving cash for the sale of their home?

Meeting these people and buying their homes requires only that you know what you want, where you want it, and what your financial options are. In other words, it requires an investment of time.

This book is designed to help you understand *all* of your options and to give you the knowledge that will enable you to finance a home creatively and responsibly. You will then be able to plan confidently and to buy wisely... no matter what your financial status may be, or how defeated you have been feeling.

For their professional and personal support, I would like to thank my very close friends: J. David Reese, general manager of McGuire Real Estate, San Francisco, California, and Jeanne Vrolyk, Century 21, Ponderosa Realty, Scotts Valley, California.

With very special thanks to my father-in-law: Senator Ollie Speraw, chairman of the board for the Century 21 Real Estate Corporation, and for Equity Loans, Long Beach, California.

1

THE AMERICAN DREAM

"The land belongs to these two:
to almighty God,
and to all his children
that have ever worked well on it."
Thomas Carlyle: *Past and Present,* 1843

OK, America, before we get started, let's ask ourselves some questions.

First, how many of you potential home buyers plan on making an "easy" million in real estate like those people you've read so much about? Just 50? Well, not everyone was born to be a real estate whiz, that's for sure.

Next, how many of you prospective first-time buyers already know that you will be able to afford a new home this year? At least 59,817 are feeling confident and optimistic. That is not too bad.

And last, how many think you will not be able to buy a home, but will keep on looking and dreaming? Wow, 5,734,952! Well, there is always hope in the land of the brave.

We buy property for any or all of the following three reasons:

1. We want room to expand, possibly because our families are growing;
2. growing equity in a home represents security; and
3. real estate is an excellent investment.

If you want to buy a home simply because you want a place to call your own, you are seeking the most fundamental joy of owning property—the *pride* of ownership. Our mundane problems seem less burdensome when the roses you planted yourself add another blossom, or when you look out of the kitchen window and see the kids building highways in their sandbox, or when a fire is blazing in the background during the Super Bowl, or when your best friend from high school comes for a visit and you have an extra room to offer your guest. Yes, owing a home can provide a great deal of fulfillment. In fact, just thinking about these things may bring to mind the security you felt growing up in your parents' home.

This sense of *security* is something that every homeowner feels immediately upon buying. But it also continues to grow with the years. Owning a home has been a saving grace for many of our parents or grandparents. The equity they have established over the years may provide their only relief as they try to subsist on Social Security and/or a minimal pension. Because the dark cloud that hangs over the Social Security system did not exist, say, 20 or 30 years ago, and because the future of our economy did not seem so ambiguous then, most people felt confident that their retirement years would be comfortable. There was not such an obvious necessity for investment as there is today. Fortunately for those who did buy homes then, they were also investing in the future.

This raises the third reason why people buy homes—it is an *investment*. Investing is regarded as a way to get ahead. Getting ahead would certainly be wonderful, but, as it is, most of us are just trying to keep even. One of Americans' biggest fears is of not having a large enough income to keep up with taxes and inflation.

Knowing that last year you were making only $1,900 a month, but now you are up to $2,200 a month, inspires a sense of pride. Gosh, you have $300 extra each month—what will you do with it? The sad reality is that you may not have any more money. Your spending power is likely to be the same as it was; a loaf of bread was $.97 then, but now is $1.08, and your monthly gas and electricity bills averaged $46 then, but now are $52. And, of course, the more you earn, the higher your tax obligation becomes.

Owning a home offers not only a hedge against inflation, as we will see, but also a tax shelter. Say that, as a renter, you are paying $450 a month for your housing. Each month that money is simply gone; by the end of the year you are $5,400 behind. Now, let's say you buy a $100,000 home. Each month your payments for housing jump to $900 a month,* and after one year you have paid out $10,800. Home values inflate at different rates depending on the area where you live, but let's say the annual average rate for your area is 13 percent. Your $100,000 home is worth $113,000 at the end of one year. Owning a home is like putting your housing payments into a savings account—plus some. That's your fight against inflation and your security for the future! And, in addition, approximately $10,000 of your payments in this example will be applied against interest due on your loan, and can be deducted from your taxable income. That's your tax shelter! You can't afford not to own! (This line of thought will be developed further in Chapter Six, "The Dollars and Sense of Buying a Home.")

Unfortunately, in days gone by, it was much easier to buy a home. If you had a steady job, you could practically walk into a lending institution, fill out an application form, and move in four weeks later. But today most housing

---

*At 13½ percent interest, a conventional loan on a $100,000 home would require monthly mortgage payments of approximately $900. This assumes that a $20,000 down payment was made at the time the house was purchased.

prices are rising 15 to 25 percent annually; we are facing fluctuating high-interest rates, housing shortages, and often a two-digit inflation rate.

So, because the world is no longer as uncomplicated as it was in the 1950s, some innovative thinking and planning—a little creativity—are in order.

First-time homebuyers, who represent a smaller and smaller proportion of today's total homebuyers (dropping in two recent years from 36 percent to 18 percent)*, especially need to leave conventional ways of thinking behind. It is time to think of other ways to finance a home purchase: through seller-financed loans, special private lenders, family support, or novel negotiating perhaps. These are just some examples of creative approaches to real estate that are working for many of today's home buyers *and* their lenders, because these methods can be shown to benefit everyone!

All you need to do is to make an investment of time before you buy your home. Analyze your finances so that you know exactly what you have to work with. Get to know the housing market in the area where you want to live—who is selling what, for how much, and where. And, finally, learn your negotiating options—both creative and conventional. Spending time on these three steps will give you the confidence it takes to buy a new home.

---

*Jack Miller, edited item, "Home Section," *San Francisco Examiner*, (1981).

2

THE ART OF GETTING WHAT YOU WANT

*"Is it not strange that desire should
so many years outlive performance?"*
Shakespeare: *Henry IV, c. 1598*

Just as we are not all painters, computer programmers, filmmakers or biochemists, neither do we all have the native ability to achieve great accomplishments in real estate. If your desire simply to own your own home is strong enough, however, you are more than capable of developing enough understanding and confidence where real estate is concerned to succeed with such a personal goal. As Woody Allen says, "80 percent of life is showing up." Unfortunately, we often tend to give ourselves too little applause for the other 20 percent.

This chapter concerns itself with three thought processes that will help you establish the positive thinking you'll need as a preparation for purchasing your home. Thinking this way will not only guarantee that you'll achieve your home-buying goal but will also help you enjoy the experience more fully.

DESIRES
Believe that it can be done! Children have an innocent, yet practical and glorious virtue: when they want something, they go after it. And they continue their pursuit even

though obstacles may slow them down; they *intend* to get what they want. The cookie jar may be on the highest shelf, or the basketball stuck underneath the neighbor's car, but the determined child will not easily bow to defeat. *Allow your desires to develop into intent.* As adults we have many desires we never pursue: "I wish I were more athletic"; "maybe I'll be promoted to office manager some day"; "I'd like to be wealthy"; "I hope I will be able to buy a home in the future." Why don't we pursue these desires with the same vitality with which we recognize them? Most often it's because we have not learned to believe one of life's most primary premises, "knock and the door shall be opened."

As adults we need to put the determination back into our goals. When our energies are directed toward a specific, well-defined aim, lesser concerns with which we busy ourselves will tend to fall away. It can be exciting and challenging to learn exactly what it is you really want from life, so try to put aside a little time each day to "let go." Spend a few moments quietly reaffirming what you want and how you are going to achieve it.

After *recognizing* your desires, the strength of your *intentions* can take over, enabling you to get what you want. And success in attaining any goal can result only from deliberately acting upon your desires.

SETTING GOALS

Setting goals can be defined as giving substance to your desires. Almost everyone plans for next summer's vacation, or for Saturday night's party, but otherwise, things just seem to happen. Many of us spend most of our time simply reacting to whatever comes our way. Life is too important to be left to chance, so set some goals!

Write your goals down. The major inner battle for most of us is desire/intent/fulfillment vs. doubt/indecision/fear.

Having a clear picture, on paper, of what you want to accomplish will help you enormously in eliminating doubt about what you intend to do.

Next, list your goals in order of priority—and don't be vague. Saying "I want to buy a home some day" is not a goal, it is merely a vague dream! Saying "I will buy a three-bedroom, 1½-bath house with a two-car garage, in a quiet neighborhood, within 20 miles of work, before 10 months have passed" is a goal! Making your goal definite, and imposing a deadline upon yourself, will help you make better plans to fulfill that goal. Once you have written them down, keep your list of goals in plain sight so that you can read them daily: "Out of sight is out of mind"; don't let your mind lose sight.

Most importantly, when setting your goals do not underestimate yourself by comparing who you are, and what you have to others. You can make the choice to do whatever you want.

A PLAN TO FULFILL YOUR GOAL

The first step toward fulfilling your goal is to make a plan. Every plan needs a beginning and an end—you know that in the end you will own a home, so now let's figure out what you are starting with:

Prepare a Financial Statement

Your financial statement should list all of your assets, your expected income, and a budget of what you spend every month. Many people have never attempted to write out an expense budget: they pay the bills, buy what they need or want, and somehow find themselves just breaking even when the next paycheck rolls in. Others, who spend according to a monthly budget, may say that by the end of the month they, too, do not have enough left over to save for anything, let alone to buy a home. Both approaches are wrong.

Your money-saving problems may not stem from your income but rather from your cash flow; when you have a priority that involves extra expenses, it comes first—not at the end of the month. So, in analyzing your monthly expenses, eliminate all the unnecessary expenditures, and put your new, high-priority expenses at the head of the list. Only then will you be able to see exactly what you're capable of. (Later on, once you know your own worth and know exactly what you will need for the home you want, you will be able to increase the amounts earmarked for other expenses.)

When you begin preparing your statement of assets and monthly income, don't permit conventional ways of thinking to paralyze you. Free your mind of all the financial limitations you're used to living with, and emphasize your financial strengths. In other words, avoid looking at such items as the ancient furnishings in your apartment, at your seven-year-old car, and at the $462 in your bank account and thinking that you have no assets. Instead, think about your great credit rating; perhaps you have a $2,000 line of credit on your Master Charge account, on which you owe nothing. Maybe there's a real-estate-agent relative in town who might give up his commission on the sale of a house to help you out. Or what about the bar stools you have been building to give away as gifts—could they be sold? Then there's all the experience you have at work; could you moonlight as a part-time consultant? Let your mind go . . . you will increase your influence over people and your surroundings by discovering more of your own worth.

Choosing a Plan of Action
Choose the course of action that would be the most *fulfill-*

ing and *effective* way to obtain your goal. Even though you are sure you could sell enough bar stools in four months to secure the extra $2,000 you've decided you'll need to accomplish your goal, it might in fact be wiser to borrow from your Master Charge account to buy the home *now* and then sell the bar stools later to pay off your loan. (This may be true if you know where you want to buy, and housing prices in that area are on their way up.) On the other hand, if your real estate uncle is willing to give up his commission, it might be better to approach him first before borrowing against a credit card, which would require you to pay interest at a high rate. Whatever action you decide upon, don't wait until the opportunity presents itself—go out and pursue the opportunity!

Accomplish your long-term goal with the help of short-term planning. After deciding which approach you are going to follow, write it out in step-by-step form. Decide what your first step will be, start working on it, accomplish it, and then move on to the next step. Though all that you do toward fulfilling your goal may not be successful, remember that if you experience any setbacks you can formulate another plan—*and you can never fail until you give up!* Learn from what doesn't work and, once again, move on. If your first plan does not work, you should not conclude that you are an unsuccessful planner, only that there is a better way to realize your goal.

Gain Knowledge

Of course, you will need to undertake a certain amount of self-education in real estate before designing your plan. This book is intended to give you enough real-estate knowledge and confidence to go out and buy. Learn with enthusiasm. You should not lack ambition when acquiring knowledge. You will find that each answered question will raise yet another *un*answered question, which, in turn, will be answered, until you feel secure enough to start making decisions. And there are many decisions to be made when negotiating a real-estate transaction. Always be patient. Don't let what you don't yet know intimidate you. Learn from whatever source is available to you. Allow others to be at your service in order to get closer to reaching your goal.

Make Decisions

During this early planning stage you should start making strong decisions, because when it comes time actually to buy your home, making the final decision can be very demanding. If others' opinions easily influence you, or you have trouble making up your mind, your decision-making skills may need some immediate attention. Think about why you are making a decision. Learn to distinguish decisions made out of stubbornness or insecurity from those made out of knowledge of your sixth sense (i.e., your reliable "gut instincts"). This ability will be a great asset when it comes to buying a home.

Avoid Procrastination and Slumps

Two of the biggest thieves waiting to rob you of success will be procrastination and personal slumps. Procrastinators are always *waiting* for the right time: what they fail to recognize, or acknowledge, is that *action* creates the right time! (And it is always better to do a little more than you think you have to in order to get the results you want.) If you tend to put things off, it is especially important for you to set your plan in motion by establishing short-term goals, as we discussed earlier. This will allow you to experience success more quickly. You will not feel so overcome by what it will take to achieve the larger goals, nor will any setbacks seem so significant that you'll feel you cannot go on.

And don't wait for achievements to change your behavior patterns. Always keep in mind that you have the right to own a home, you deserve it, and you can make the choice to get what you want . . . *and* that there will never be a better time to buy real estate than now!

The second thief is represented by those times when we are "just down." This is known as being in a slump—a time when we don't show the same enthusiasm for life that we usually do. It is easy to foresee the arrival of a slump: its warning signals include tiredness, a sense of pressure, negativity, inflexibility and resistance to change. When you feel a slump stealing your energy, put up a fight. This will demand a certain amount of determination. Do only the work you enjoy, and avoid activities you dislike that may tend to lower your self-esteem. You may love hammering nails, but hate fixing the automobile. So if the car needs work and the roof needs repair, get out the ladder and work on the roof. In fact, it is a good time to get out into some fresh air. Also, try offering yourself a few nice rewards, like a banana split. The old saying that the spirits of a depressed woman can easily be lifted by buying a new hat, is true! Be good to yourself.

Making the Commitment
Make a commitment *to do* what you want done! Despite the hopes and promises people make to themselves, most have a tendency to act in accordance with their fears. To avoid this, the commitment must be total and be backed by persistence. Implementation of the points just discussed in this chapter cannot be based on a concept of good luck. Every successful person knows that *life will give you what you want if you go after it.* Even if success comes so slowly that you feel as if you are climbing a spiral staircase, having a clear understanding of this philosophy for suc-

cess will increase the enjoyment and greatly reduce the problems and headaches of purchasing a home. With your total commitment, every step of your planning will bring a little more of tomorrow's dreams closer to today.

In 1955 George S. Clason wrote a very short inspirational book entitled *The Richest Man in Babylon*, about how the richest man in Babylon acquired his wealth. The book presents a step-by-step method to help one realize a richer future. One of the ten steps set forth is: "Be thine own landlord." The book is an interesting and thought-provoking approach to financial planning, and I highly recommend it.

3

INTRODUCING THE MONEY MARKET

Real-estate financing is using real property as collateral to pay back a loan.

Buying real-estate "creatively" has been a necessary development born of hard economic times. But this does not mean that such creative buying is a more difficult approach to buying real estate than the use of conventional methods. Nor is creative buying only for the buyer who is most pressed financially. In fact, being creative can be beneficial in any real-estate purchase. And during times of tight money and high interest rates, the market actually favors those who buy creatively.

Just how favorable the housing market is going to be for the buyer to purchase a home using creative finance methods is determined by the mood of the seller. When plenty of money is available at the banks and their interest rates are lower (which makes it easier for a buyer to qualify for a loan), it is more likely a seller will ask for all his or her equity in cash at the time the home is sold. And easier economic times produce many eager buyers, so the seller's mood becomes less flexible. After all, if there are a large number of buyers knocking on the door, why should a seller consider negotiating with you?

On the other hand, during harder times (when money is less available), the seller's mood changes, and he or she may be anxious to negotiate a creative sale: when buyers are scarce, a seller will become flexible—just to sell.

Ah, do I suddenly hear a few prayers for a dip in the economy, lasting just long enough for you to buy a house? (Don't worry, a buyer's market is likely to dominate the 80s. However, housing costs will continue to rise, especially as interest rates drop.)

The relationship among available monies, interest rates, and inflation is complicated, of course, but all home buyers should master the basics. Here is a simplified explanation of our money system so you can see how it affects the housing market:

The major cause of inflation is an increase in the amount of money printed and put into circulation by the government. When this happens, money becomes worth less, resulting in a continual rise in the prices of all goods. The presence of this extra money also tends to increase our spending, thus causing a higher demand for goods, and again driving prices higher. Banks are affected in the same way. When money becomes less valuable, lenders need to impose higher interest rates, which are based not only on the lender's profit margin but also on a projection of the future value of money.

Where does the money come from for conventional housing loans? Savings and loan companies and banks are the primary lenders; they can loan up to 85 percent of the money they have on deposit—your money. These lenders also loan money that they in turn borrow from the Federal Reserve Bank. However, to curb inflation, the Federal Reserve Bank restricts the flow of money, by raising *their* interest rates. Thus it costs more for banks to borrow, and the higher interest rates are passed on to the home buyer. The result? A tight-money market.

With every increase in interest rates, it becomes much more difficult for a home buyer to qualify for a home loan (because the home buyer's monthly mortgage payments will, of course, be higher). This, coupled with the generally high cost of housing, causes some staggering current statistics: for instance, 61 percent of first-time home buyers need two incomes to qualify for a home mortgage loan.

Before discussing creative financing approaches to buying real estate, let's first summarize what is considered a conventional approach.

CONVENTIONAL LOAN SOURCES

Generally, in a conventional financing arrangement the buyer advances 20 percent of the purchase price as a down payment and then has a conventional lending institution finance the remaining 80 percent. You have a fair chance of qualifying for a conventional loan if the home costs no more than approximately two and one-half times your annual gross income (including the 20 percent down payment). For example, to buy a $100,000 home, you will need $20,000 down and a yearly gross income of $40,000.

Such conventional lending institutions include commercial banks, state or federally chartered savings and loan companies (they are "federal" if the word is somewhere in the name), and mortgage companies.

Commercial banks have been in the business of making long-term home loans (although it is a smaller portion of their lending business), with payments amortized over a 20-to-30 year period at the highest prevailing interest rates. But recently, because the state of the economy has become so unpredictable, banks are hesitant to make long-term, fixed-rate loans. Long-term loans are becoming obsolete. In the past, interest rates moved up slowly, with only slight fluctuations. And in California, for example, where houses change ownership on an average of every six years, the banks were able to increase the interest rates when the terms on a home's mortgage loan were rewritten for each new buyer. However, the Wellenkamp decision, the result of a court case, requires these lenders (including state chartered savings and loan companies), to let the new owner *assume* the original loan with no increase in the interest rate. (Read about loan assumptions in "Creative Financing Methods" later in this chapter.) These lenders then began to create new loan concepts, such as short-term loans, renegotiable-rate mortgages, variable interest rates and adjustable mortgage loans. These new loan terms give the lenders the right to increase the interest rates periodically or to make the loan fully due and payable on a given date, all depending upon the terms of the loan.

Commercial banks will loan up to 90 percent of the purchase price if the borrower is considered an excellent credit risk and if the property value is high. However, most conventional loans are for 70 to 80 percent of the home's purchase price; for these loans, buyers usually must have a good credit standing, advance a down payment of 20 percent of the purchase price, and have a gross monthly income three times the monthly payment of the loan. (Lenders, however, are becoming more flexible about these conditions. If other monthly bills are low, some lenders will allow a home mortgage payment to be as high as 35 to 40 percent of the borrower's net income.)

Savings and loan companies offer loans similar to those of commercial banks, with the majority of their investments being real-estate home loans. Usually these companies will loan 80 percent of the appraised price or of the selling price, whichever is lower, at prevailing interest rates.

When arranging a loan with a savings and loan company (as with a commercial bank), make sure your loan can be assumed by a future buyer when you sell your home. NOTE: "Federal" savings and loan companies do not allow straight assumptions, but there are creative financial approaches to skirt these rules. However, in light of the new adjustable rate mortgage (ARM), federal savings and loan companies soon may allow assumptions, because interest rates would no longer be fixed for these institutions. (Read about ARM, as well as the other new loan terms regarding interest rates discussed above, in Chapter Six.)

Mortgage bankers are involved with private lenders, government loans (such as FHA and VA loans), and commercial banks and savings and loan companies. The size of the loan and the interest rates will vary depending on the lending source. Mortgage bankers are more or less middlemen, and they specialize in obtaining loans usually from one or two sources (for example, one specific major bank and the FHA).

Mortgage bankers match borrowers and lenders and also service their accounts. They differ from mortgage *brokers*, who simply bring borrower and lender together for a set fee. (Mortgage brokers are also called hard-money lenders: their loan terms will be the stiffest and they write loans with the highest interest rates and with short payback periods.)

Insurance companies supply long-term financing for high-yield, low-risk investments such as real estate. However, these home mortgage loans are at present not applicable to the individual home buyer. Insurance companies participate only in very large investments, usually commercial and/or loans over $1 million. A few insurance corporations have branched out to create mortgage companies, but they are not directly affiliated with the insurance activities as such.

Other conventional lending sources are few and obscure. Some universities, for example, have endowment trust funds and make home-mortgage loans. But these lending situations are very limited and are not worth searching for.

NOTE: In the past the only home-mortgage lending sources were those mentioned above. They were the conventional lenders who also wrote two "unconventional" financing packages: FHA loans and VA loans. However, with the many approaches to financing a home available today, FHA loans and VA loans now are considered conventional:

FHA stands for the Federal Housing Administration. It insures loans by approved financial institutions. The loan size is regulated, but the maximum amount that can be loaned increases as the cost of housing rises (check with a real-estate agent or qualified lender to get the current maximum loan size). The interest rates are federally adjusted and fluctuate at a level slightly lower than prevailing market rates, with a minimal down payment required. (The down-payment amount changes, but to give you an idea of what to expect, it is currently 3 percent of the first $25,000 of the purchase price; 5 percent of the excess purchase price over $25,000; and 100 percent of the purchase price over the FHA appraisal price.)

There are qualifications for buyers, which include restrictions on obtaining second-mortgage financing, and the requirement that monthly net income be approximately four times the amount of monthly mortgage payments. Sellers often avoid selling to buyers who are trying to finance the purchase with a FHA loan, because the sellers are required to pay "points." Points represent a loan fee determined by the percentage difference between the lower FHA interest rate and the prevailing market interest rates; FHA rates are always lower. If the difference is 4 percent, then the seller must pay 4 percent of the entire loan to the lender. This is an expense to the seller as it is illegal for buyers to pay the points. (For example, on a $75,000 home purchase, points at 4 percent would equal $3,000.)

VA (Veterans Administration) loans are handled by the same lenders who deal in FHA loans. The VA insures its own loans, which are available only to qualified veterans. No down payment is required on a VA loan; however, the buyer is required to pay 100 percent of the purchase price over the VA appraisal price as a down payment. Maximum loan amounts and interest rates change with the economy, so check with a qualified VA lender or your agent.

Qualifications for buyers include the requirement that monthly income be four times the amount of monthly mortgage payments; also, the buyer must occupy the home. Interest rates usually are lower than prevailing market rates, but the "point system" is the same with a VA loan as it is with a FHA loan.

A buyer does not have to be a veteran to assume a VA loan, but should a veteran allow his or her VA loan to be assumed, that veteran will lose VA loan eligibility and not be able to obtain another VA loan when purchasing a new home.

If you are a veteran, I encourage you to investigate a VA home-mortgage loan.

CREATIVE FINANCING METHODS

The following is a summary of creative finance methods you can use when buying a home. These are alternative approaches to financing; alternative ways to find cash, and ways to avoid the need for cash when purchasing your home. Use of these creative finance methods in actual real-estate transactions are described throughout the book in subsections entitled "Creativity in Action."

First, let's discuss the term "creative financing." Creativity (in fields other than the arts) usually arises from demand, and this is true of real estate. New methods of financing the purchase of a home have been "created" so Americans could keep pace with the economy. These methods are all valid, legal and very practical for today's home buyer. But "creative financing" has also received critical comment in the media because the term often has been associated with short-term loans due during high interest rate times. The higher the interest rates, the more difficult it is for a home owner to refinance in order to pay in full the loan that has come due. Higher interest rates constitute higher monthly payments and, in turn, a greater percentage of the homeowner's monthly income.

When homeowners cannot afford to refinance and/or qualify for refinancing, the number of foreclosures skyrocket. This has been happening in many parts of the country in the early 1980s.

Short-term loans, however, are just part of the many new, creative loan possibilities that have become beneficial breakthroughs for all potential home buyers. But it is very important to buy *responsibly,* no matter what financing method you decide upon. So, as you read and make decisions about buying your own home, keep in mind these two points:

1. Make sure you can comfortably afford the monthly payments and that you have the resources to meet the qualifications for refinancing or paying off any short-term loans when they come due.
2. When you buy, never assume or finance a mortgage loan that will come due inside three years. When refinancing, most lenders will loan only 70 to 80 per-

cent of the home's appraised value; therefore, it is
necessary to have a good amount of equity in the
home before applying for the new loan (especially
when a minimal down payment has been made).

Assumption of an existing loan is the first option a creative home buyer should look for to avoid *having to qualify
for* a new loan through a conventional lender. Say you are
interested in buying a home for $100,000, and the existing
loan balance is $65,000 (in other words, the seller still owes
the bank $65,000; the remaining $35,000 is the seller's
equity). To assume the loan means that the home buyer
takes over primary responsibility to repay that loan, under
all its terms, but does not have to qualify as a borrower
under a new loan.

It is becoming mandatory in increasing numbers of
states for lenders to allow assumption on their loans.
Major lenders are not trying to stop such loan assumption
because the burden is on the lender to prove that payment
of the loan would be threatened by the new buyer.

Second and third mortgages have traditionally indicated that
the homeowner is having financial problems; today they
are a sign of creativity and are becoming more and more
common. Let's consider the example of the home selling
for $100,000 discussed above. If you are to assume the
$65,000 *first*-mortgage loan, where is the other $35,000 to
come from? One creative financing approach would be to
ask the seller to carry the *second*-mortgage loan for the
remaining $35,000, or at least a portion of that amount.
The buyer would then make payments on the first-
mortgage loan to the original bank, and on the second-
mortgage loan to the seller. There are a wide range of
negotiating possibilities using second mortgages, as you

will read in the "Creativity in Action" stories.

Acquiring a third mortgage (or even a fourth or a fifth mortgage) takes this process one step further. Say the seller will let you owe him or her part of the $35,000, but not all of it. You then can seek a third source for the remaining funds. It is even possible to assume an already existing second mortgage and negotiate with the seller to carry a third mortgage.

There are many sources of second and third mortgages: the seller, private lenders (found through real-estate offices or similar connections), hard-money lenders (found by going to specialized finance firms such as mortgage brokers), family, company credit unions—just about anyone loaning money. NOTE: As mentioned earlier, the terms of hard-money lenders, such as mortgage brokers, are the stiffest, and their services are best used as a last resort.

Carrying a second mortgage can be advantageous to the seller. Do your best to discover the seller's future plans. The seller may be retiring and prefer a monthly income, or may prefer a tax advantage by receiving only part of his or her equity in cash right away. First, check with your realtor or tax consultant before suggesting any of these options to the seller. It even may be to the seller's benefit to waive your payments for a period of time or to accept payments of interest only with the entire principal balance due on the payback date; both approaches are commonly used.

Second- or third-mortgage lenders will determine your loan payments by amortizing the loan over a long period (anywhere from 10 to 40 years) with the balance (known as a balloon payment) usually due within three to seven years. The interest rates are flexible, depending on the lender, and some lenders will take interest-only payments, with the entire balance due on the payback date. Payment of interest only can be to the buyer's advantage, as it gage interest payments are tax-deductible, whereas payments of principal are not. Be sure to shop several lenders because their fees and interest rates will vary.

If the second- or third-mortgage lender makes loans on a regular basis, and depending on the size of the loan, the lender probably will ask the borrower to fill out a standard application form to ensure that the borrower can make the payments on all the mortgages. Mortgage holders understandably must protect themselves against default on mortgage payments. If a home is foreclosed, the first-mortgage holder is paid first from whatever monies are received from the sale of the home; then the second-mortgage holder is paid and so on.

If the home were heavily mortgaged, of course (for example, if little or no money had been advanced as a down payment, and if the home's entire value were mortgaged), the holder of the last mortgage could lose money. If you must complete application forms for one or two subsequent loans, and if you feel you may have trouble qualifying for any of the loans, there always is room for negotiation; even finding a financially responsible cosigner may be your answer.

Wrap-around/all-inclusive trust deeds also have been gaining popularity. For example, a house is for sale at $100,000. The seller has an existing loan for $70,000 at 11 percent interest and is willing to carry the second-mortgage financing on the remaining $30,000. The $70,000 loan is "wrapped" (combined) with the $30,000 by the seller at 13.5 percent interest. The buyer then makes one payment per month to the seller (at an interest rate which would still be below that available to a new first loan). In turn, the seller continues to make the necessary payments on the original loan. But the seller not only collects 13.5 percent on the $30,000, due him or her, but also reaps the interest difference between 11 percent and 13.5 percent for the monthly payments owed the bank.

This type of financing is attractive to the buyer in that it can offer full (or near full) financing, with good payment terms, without the buyer having to qualify for a new loan. Yet the property title is recorded in the buyer's name and the buyer has total rights to the property. However, the seller still is primarily responsible for the original loan, and should the buyer default, the seller would have to go through complete foreclosure proceedings to regain possession.

A seller might want to negotiate a wrap-around loan because the buyer cannot easily qualify for a new loan, has only a minimal down payment, or because there is a lack of time to pursue new financing. The seller may insist on obtaining a top price, but be willing to offer good terms in exchange.

However, here is a special *sellers beware* note: you should not allow an agent or anyone else to suggest this be your approach. Sellers usually want to finance wrap-around loans when they are anxious to sell *and* because of the bonus to them in keeping the difference between the bank's interest rate on the first mortgage and the interest rate they charge the buyer on the whole package. For one or both of these reasons, sellers may be motivated to lower the selling price of the home, since they would recover any loss therefrom in the extra interest payments they would be receiving over the years.

So it's all set. The wrap-around loan is signed, and then here's what some buyers do: They go directly to the bank that holds the first mortgage and they *assume* that loan at the original lower interest rate. Then they go out and refinance the second mortgage and pay off the sellers (because a prepayment-penalty clause was not part of the wrap-around loan agreement). The sellers not only lose the years of interest earnings they were expecting, but also they were "tricked" into selling their home for a lower price. (This is a fairly common ploy by quick-thinking buyers. The same thing often happens on car lots: Buyers motivate the car dealer to sell at a low price by letting them carry the financing with a high interest rate; then the buyer pays cash a few days later.)

Contract for sale/land contracts are openly and commonly used in some areas of the country. Under the terms of the contract the buyer makes an agreed down payment, takes possession of the home and makes payments on the balance of the existing loan to the seller (although occasionally the payments can be made directly to the lender). Title to the home remains in the seller's name, so should the buyer default, it would take only a "quiet-title" (a simple court action that establishes title) for the seller to regain possession (as the seller still is primarily responsible for the loan). The buyer should try to avoid an "acceleration clause" in the contract so a future buyer could assume the contract: an "acceleration clause" means the balance accelerates upon resale and becomes due immediately. Also, the contract must specify that the seller cannot encumber the property further.

This method of financing is used so that the buyer will not have to qualify for the loan as if it were new. For this reason the contract never is officially recorded (however, recording the title from such contracts is common in some states and is openly accepted by the lenders). In other words, this method is a roundabout way of assuming a loan; but where loan assumptions are allowed, the method is less desirable as an option.

Whether recorded or not, contract for sale/land contracts are completely legal, with full risk of "being discovered" going to the buyer. Many real-estate company agreement forms now include clauses holding both the company and the seller free of responsibility when such financing approaches are used. If the buyer is discovered by the original lender (this can happen when the tax assessor statements are sent to the lender, or when insurance policies are rewritten and notices are sent to the lender), then it is the buyer's responsibility to establish a new loan.

When entering into this type of contract, be sure you understand all the legal points involved: What happens when the buyer wants to sell? What happens if the seller can't present a clear title at the closing? Consult a competent real-estate attorney.

Subject-to contracts are very similar to contract for sale/land contracts, except that the buyer takes title to the home. Use of these contracts avoids the need to requalify with a lender, and the buyer is at risk should the lender discover that the home has been sold. (But as mentioned above, some lenders accept this financing method and do not contest it.) Even though the buyer takes title (and whether or not the buyer pays the bank directly) the buyer has assumed only secondary liability for payment of the loan; the seller still is primarily responsible.

Just as the contract for sale/land contract is more advantageous to the seller, the subject-to contract is more advantageous to the buyer. Should the buyer default, the seller would have to go through complete foreclosure proceedings to regain title to the home, and in the meantime would have to make all outstanding payments on the home in order to retain interest in the property. (This is especially true if little or no down payment was made on the home and if the seller is the holder of any secondary mortgages.) Consult a qualified real-estate agent or someone competent in real-estate law before considering a subject-to contract.

Lease/purchase options become popular during hard economic times. The buyer enters into a lease/purchase option with the intention of buying the home within a certain period of time. A buyer might want a lease now with the option to buy later because he or she may not qualify for a loan just now, because the interest rate on the existing loan may be relatively low, and in the hope that mortgage interest rates will be lower than at the time of the lease agreement when he or she must decide whether to pick up the option to buy.

As with all real-estate contracts, the terms of a lease/purchase option can be negotiated. The following is a general overview: The buyer usually advances a minimal deposit, which can be a portion or all of an agreed down payment. The buyer then makes payments to the seller to cover the seller's current loan expenses. The buyer does not take title to the property; however, a lease/purchase option agreement should be recorded to keep the owner from further encumbering the property. The buyer benefits most by having a guaranteed sales price and not having to qualify for a new loan. Commonly, when the option to buy is exercised, the buyer assumes the first mortgage loan and the seller carries the second mortgage loan which covers their equity.

While the lease/purchase option contract is in effect, the buyer may or may not also make interest-only payments to the seller on their equity. And the buyer may or may not pay property taxes and insurance fees. Depending on these terms, the buyer may be allowed to take the deductions from his taxable income, rather than the seller.

It is particularly important here to make sure that all the paperwork is done properly. Verify that your option to purchase is clear and unencumbered. And understand the provisions for resale of the home should you decide to move before the lease/purchase option period has ended.

Consult a real-estate lawyer before signing a lease/ purchase option contract.

Buy-down is a term used when a loan's high interest rate is subsidized by a private party. This private party would most likely be the seller, the builder, or a relative of the buyer.

Say you want to buy a home but there are no assumable loans available to you. This means you must qualify for a new mortgage loan, but because of high interest rates, you may not qualify for the loan. In that case here's what can happen: A builder often will attract buyers to new homes by advertising loans available with substantially lower-than-market interest rates. This is a creative-financing lure; on a new loan for $75,000, at an interest rate of 17 percent, the builder will pay the lender in advance the difference between the amount due at 17 percent and that due at a lower interest rate—say 13 percent—for a three-to-five year period. (At an interest rate of 13 percent, it is much easier for a buyer to qualify for a mortgage loan because the monthly payments would be approximately $240 less than on a loan at 17 percent interest. Depending on the market, the builder may add this amount to the sale price.) At the end of this period, the buyer must make payments at the higher interest rate. Hopefully the buy-down period will end at a time when it is easier for the buyer to pay at that rate or when lower rates are available.

Use of this buy-down method was started by builders who sell large home divisions. Bankers were eager to work with builders on these large deals, but not so eager to offer buy-downs for sales of smaller, individual home units— that is, until Fannie Mae! Fannie Mae, the Federal National Mortgage Association, is the country's largest home-mortgage lender, having purchased over $60 billion worth of loans. Fannie Mae purchases home loans from every type of lender, and Fannie Mae's activities often affect the housing-finance market. (Your home loan may be serviced by a local lender but owned by Fannie Mae even without your knowledge.)

Fannie Mae now purchases mortgages with buy-down agreements from local lenders. It will buy loans at rates no more than 3 percent below prevailing interest rates, for a period of not more than five years. These loans can be subsidized, for example, by the builder, who may pay the subsidy in advance with no repayment necessary, or possibly by an individual seller who may hold a second mortgage on the home and be repaid, for example, at the end of a three-to-five year period. (As an alternative, the seller may pay the buy-down sum to the bank in exchange for the buyer's payment of the seller's full asking price for the home, or a price slightly above what the seller is asking.)

With Fannie Mae willing to purchase buy-downs, more and more local lenders will be willing to offer mortgage loans using this creative method. And sellers and buyers will be able to negotiate toward a more attractive finance program for the buyer when no assumable loans are available to him or her. In that light, this buy-down method may even be applied to second- or third-mortgage loans in private transactions when first-mortgage loans are assumable.

Cobuyers are two or more buyers purchasing the same home. A cobuyer could be a friend, a relative, a business associate. Many cobuyers are single adults copurchasing condominiums in urban areas, or they are families co-purchasing larger homes in order to share the cost of housing. For families cobuying, duplexes are particularly attractive, since they allow the cost- sharing of down payments and mortgage payments on a single structure, yet still give each family its own separate living space. Builders, especially builders of condominiums, are becoming sensitive to the needs of cobuyers; for example, the builders are designing homes with two master bedrooms.

If you decide to cobuy, go beyond the usual paperwork to avoid any personal or legal disputes that can, and often do, occur. Have a real-estate attorney draw up the agreement. Here are some questions to consider:

1. What if one of the parties cannot pay their share of the mortgage payments, insurance, or taxes for a period of time due to financial difficulties?
2. What if one party is forced to move (for example, because of a relocation)? How would the selling price and terms be determined? Would the other party have first-right-of-refusal? Or would the party vacating be allowed to rent their half?
3. What are the financial agreements on building and property maintenance? (Say one party wants to fence in the yard and the other does not; or the roof needs reshingling and only one party can afford the cost for this.)

Finally, make sure the property deed specifies your coownership as "tenants in common," not "joint tenancy." Coownership as tenants in common allows you to will your half of the property to whomever you wish and also to sell whenever you choose. (If your cobuyer is a close relative, this may not be advisable, however. Check into this with a real-estate lawyer).

Alternative lending companies match investors with prospective homeowners. These companies are new and altogether different from hard-money mortgage firms or mortgage bankers.

Typically, the prospective homeowner has very little money for a down payment and has trouble qualifying for a mortgage loan. Alternative lending companies help these home buyers by finding an investor who will put up a substantial sum of money as a down payment, with the investor's name entered on the home's title as cobuyer. The home buyer then moves into the home and makes all loan payments for a period of one to five years. The investor then is repaid the down payment plus a percentage of the increased value of the home—often 50 percent. The investor's split in the profit will be determined by how much was originally invested. Paying the investor often is done by refinancing, or, unfortunately, by selling. If using an investor, try to have the investment period extended as long as possible so a substantial amount of equity in the home can be built up.

An altogether different approach taken by an alternative lending company uses three creative financing methods but without using private investors. For example, such a lending company will *assume* the existing first-mortgage loan on the home and then *wrap* it with the *second-mortgage* financing, which they will provide. These companies can write a fully assumable, fixed-interest-rate, 30-year loan that can be passed on to future buyers. Sounds very creative and almost too good to be true, right? But these companies do exist. They make their money by charging points (for example, 4 percent of the home's selling price) and by charging a currently prevailing interest rate on the entire loan. By making payments on the first-mortgage loan, which they have assumed, they can keep the difference between the interest rate they are collecting and that given to the first-mortgage holder (as described in the section on wrap arounds/all-inclusive trust deeds).

Alternative lending companies are cropping up everywhere—but still they may be difficult to find. Asking your local realtor or title company if there are alternative lending companies in your area. Be sure to check their background and references; these companies are new, but some are more reputable than others.

Before using an alternative lender, consider your financial alternatives. You probably will have lower monthly payments with an alternative lender, but sharing equity the first few years you own the home undoubtedly will be more costly to you in the end. If you use a hard-money lender (a mortgage broker), your monthly payments will be higher, but you will pay less in the long run. Discuss all possibilities with a qualified third person, such as a lawyer or real-estate agent.

Who is SAM? SAM is the federal government's Shared Appreciation Mortgage plan to help the first-time home buyer. SAM and similar approaches, such as using an alternative lender who uses an investor as a cobuyer, are sure to be popular in the future.

Under a SAM loan, the lender substantially lowers the interest rate—say from 15 to 10 percent. This greatly reduces monthly payments which in turn helps some people to qualify for the loan. However, within a specified period of time the buyer must sell or refinance in order to pay the lender a percentage of the increased home value—in other words, split the equity with the lender. In essence, the lender becomes a temporary cobuyer.

A *subescrow* is a creative maneuver to avoid certain lender rules that reject second- and third-mortgage financing. When a buyer approaches a conventional lender for a new first-mortgage loan—say for 80 percent of the purchase price—the lender may not approve the loan unless the buyer can pay the remaining 20 percent in cash. This always is the case with FHA loans. Since these lenders require that no second mortgage can "concurrently record" with the first mortgage, many escrow companies will have a subescrow record two days to two weeks after the close of escrow. This subescrow then will include second- and possibly third-mortgage lenders. PLEASE NOTE that this is commonly done in many areas but is fraudulent nonetheless. Lenders usually are not told that there is to be a subescrow arrangement, or they hear of it but allow it to happen without receiving formal notification.

Family support could be a major form of relief for many first-time home buyers. Approaching family is often a last resort for home buyers because it may be difficult for them to ask relatives for financial assistance. But it could easily be to the relatives' benefit (and joy) to lend a hand; after all, money invested in real estate is particularly well placed. However, before asking a family member for money, know exactly what assets you have and what you will need, so that the discussion can be centered around those exact needs.

Also consider any foreseen inheritance. Being able to help now, when you most need it, would most likely bring more pleasure to someone close to you, than leaving the money to you in their will.

* * *

There are other terms for the creative financing options just discussed, such as "installment sales," but they simply are alternate names for, or variations of, these methods. As you read each of the "Creativity in Action" stories in this book, you will become familiar with how homes can be bought using these financing methods.

A Word About Down Payments
You may have some money saved, or a large sum of money

coming to you soon, which you want to advance as a down payment on a home—it would be a good investment of your money. But even if you do not have the cash right now, there are alternate ways for you to make a down payment. Here are a few simple suggestions:

1. Offer personal property—a boat, a car, stocks, etc.—instead of cash.
2. Take a loan on your life-insurance policy.
3. Borrow by using a major credit card (if you don't have one, apply for it now).
4. Borrow from a private lender, establishing a second- or third-mortgage loan, and use that money as a down payment.
5. There may be work that needs completing on the home before the close of escrow (termite repairs, landscaping, home repairs). By doing it yourself you may earn a reduction in the down payment.
6. Your real estate agent may take a note (an IOU) from you in lieu of his or her commission (especially if the agent feels the sale may not be completed otherwise); this may enable you to make the down payment.

It would be wonderful if the home's amenities—such as the floor plan—could once again become the greatest priority in choosing a home. But it appears that, at least for a few more years, the ability to simply finance the home will be more important. So, along with understanding conventional money sources, it will be your ability to deal creatively that will enable you to buy your new home.

CREATIVITY IN ACTION
Mr. and Mrs. Martin lived in their home for nearly 30 years. They bought the house when it was new, and after raising a

family, they decided to move to a smaller place. Sharon Woods wanted to buy their home.

In the 1950s, the Martins paid $25,000 for their home, but now their firm asking price was $100,000. When Sharon Woods met the sellers, she learned that the original bank loan was assumable. This meant that she could take over the small payments of the original loan at a low, fixed-interest rate.

There was approximately $11,000 to pay on that assumable loan, so now all Sharon had to worry about was the other $89,000! She asked the Martins if they would be interested in taking on a second-mortgage loan—that is, after Sharon made a small down payment, the sellers would carry the balance, which would allow Sharon to make monthly payments on the remainder.

Their answer was no. Sharon immediately asked why. (Remember, you never know what the seller's situation really is, and often they accept offers that surprise everyone, including their own real-estate agent. Always ask why. Never end your pursuit until all avenues of negotiation have been considered.)

The Martins had responded with a no based on the frustration and confusion that is common among many retired people today. Even though the Martins had $89,000 equity in their home, they had been living on Social Security for a year now and were having trouble making ends meet. Inflation affecting property taxes, utility rates, food prices, etc., was not allowing them to maintain a home properly on such a small income. So they had decided to sell their home and live more comfortably from their equity, in a rental home.

This was a major mistake for the Martins, and Sharon knew it. She made the Martins a new offer. Sharon would pay $95,000 for the home ($5,000 less than the asking price), with a $10,000 down payment. She would assume the original loan of $11,000, and the Martins would carry the second mortgage on the remaining $69,000, on which Sharon would make interest-only payments for five years. At the end of those five years the balance on the second mortgage would be due.

Negotiations continued. As they talked, Sharon explained to the sellers that by taking the $10,000 down payment they would easily be able to rebuy into a nice smaller home—say, a mobile home, or possibly a condominium. The total in interest-only payments they would receive over the next five years (at 13 percent interest) would be $44,850. That's about $750 a month, an amount that would amply cover their new home's loan costs. This also would leave the money they would receive from Social Security for other expenses and enable them to raise their standard of living. Also, they would reestablish equity in a new-home purchase, and in five years the balance of $69,000 still would be theirs, not to mention the tax benefits of owning.

The obvious gain for Sharon was that she could move into a $100,000 home (for $95,000) on her own, with minimal money down. Sharon knew that making interest-only payments at the rate she was offering the Martins was a better financial package than she would find elsewhere. Also, in five years, the home would be worth approximately $50,000 more (based on the rising home prices in the area), and that refinancing the loan to pay the $69,000 would be easy.

Unfortunately, making payments on both loans (the first loan of $11,000, and the second-mortgage loan of $69,000), would take half of Sharon's net monthly income—about $1,000. Even though this sum included taxes and insurance, it is a high percentage of one's income to pay for housing. But Sharon had no other large bills and she knew this would be a comfortable financial arrangement for her lifestyle.

The Martins accepted the offer, and Sharon moved in 30 days later.

4

WHEN IT'S CHEAPER AND EASIER

Real estate brings security through it's guaranteed future value.
                                    Anonymous

TODAY'S HOUSING MARKET

The number of would-be home buyers in the United States increases steadily each year. And the demand for new homes continues to outpace construction. There is, as a result, no doubt that real estate will remain one of the most secure hedges against inflation throughout the 1980s and, it seems likely, far beyond the end of this decade. The construction of new homes is recovering slightly after a major slack in the early 1980s, the worst period since the immediate post-World War II era. But new homes are being built at only one fourth the rate of five years ago and the steady demand for new homes exceeds the number of homes currently under construction by over one million. (The main cause again is those infamously high interest rates.) This demand for something that is in short supply continues to drive prices up.

But changes are in the offing. By 1990 our concept of the typical American family home—a three-bedroom house with a two-car garage—will be passé. No specific living situation will be considered typical. Single-family dwellings may continue to be regarded as the ideal, but the practicality of condominiums, cooperative housing, time-shared second homes for vacations, and other forms of housing will each become more and more common.

At the same time, home prices will reach all-time highs during the 1980s. As hope for a revival in the construction of rental housing continues to wane, buying will become an increasing necessity. Rentals are becoming harder to find, with the condominium and time-sharing concepts catching on fast; it has become much more financially advantageous for developers to sell individual units within a large structure, rather than selling entire new buildings for a landlord's rental purposes. This means that the resale market (the turnover of homes that already exist) now is dominating the housing market. Seventy-five percent of the market is resale property, and a limited product always is expensive.

Because Americans tend to move to areas with warm climates and prospering industry, most real estate is purchased, and prices are highest, in the country's southern and western regions. (Population shifts also are occurring within these areas; this will be discussed in the following chapter.)

The following chart shows the percentage of *resale* homes sold in each of the country's four main regions. The chart demonstrates that where there is a demand for housing, the prices are high; the best example is in the West, where only 19 percent of the country's resale homes were sold, but also where the buyers paid 26 percent of the total monies spent on resale housing.

SEASONAL AND LONG-TERM HOUSING TRENDS

Although there are definite seasonal and long-term housing trends, there has not been a drop in median housing prices in the United States, even through the past three recessions. When there are annual real estate "lows" and occasional economic recessions, housing prices may stabi-

Region	Volume percent of existing single-family-home sales	Dollar percent spent on single-family-home sales
Northeast (Pa., N.Y., N.J., R.I., Conn., Mass., Vt., N.H., Me.)	14	14
North-Central (N.D., S.D., Neb., Kans., Ia., Mo., Minn., Ill., Ohio, Ind., Wis., Mich.)	29	24
South (Tex., Okla., Ark., La., Miss., Ala., Tenn., Ky., Ga., Fla., S.C., N.C., W. Va., Va., Md., Del.)	38	36
West (Wash., Oreg., Calif., Ala., Idaho, Nev., Ariz., Utah, Mont., Wyo., Colo., N.M., Hawaii)	19	26
	100	100

(These figures were supplied by the National Board of Realtors and then were averaged over a five-year period (1976–80). The West's 19 percent volume rate has become a higher percentage in the more recent years, and the chart does not reflect the percentage of *new*-home sales in that area.)

The two charts on this page give an overview of housing prices across the country. They indicate not only the current costs, but also in which areas costs are likely to continue climbing the fastest. [These charts were printed in *U.S. News and World Report* in the late summer of 1981.]

How Home-Lot Prices Compare

New figures on land values show that it's not construction costs alone that inflate the prices of new homes across the U.S.

According to American University's Homer Hoyt Institute, finished residential lots averaged $13,539 nationwide in 1980—up $4,592 over four years earlier.

Here is how the states ranked in average costs of residential lots per square foot—

	Cost Per Square Foot	Change From 1976
Dist. of Columbia	$11.39	*
Hawaii	$10.38	*
California	$ 3.68	+134%
Alaska	$ 3.00	*
Nevada	$ 1.82	+231%
Illinois	$ 1.82	+ 67%
Wyoming	$ 1.80	*
Oregon	$ 1.75	+127%
Colorado	$ 1.70	+ 79%
Maryland	$ 1.48	+ 38%
Utah	$ 1.45	+ 67%
Virginia	$ 1.42	+ 63%
Louisiana	$ 1.34	+120%
Arizona	$ 1.28	+374%
Washington	$ 1.25	+102%
Ohio	$ 1.18	+ 82%
Texas	$ 1.18	+ 71%
Florida	$ 1.18	+ 24%
Idaho	$ 1.16	+132%
Kansas	$ 1.14	+ 52%
Nebraska	$ 1.13	+ 64%
New Mexico	$ 1.13	+ 57%
New Jersey	$ 1.11	+ 41%
U.S. average	**$ 1.05**	**+ 36%**
Montana	$ 1.04	+ 33%
Missouri	$ 1.01	+ 28%
Oklahoma	$ 1.00	+ 70%
Iowa	$ 1.00	+ 33%
Minnesota	$ .99	+106%
Michigan	$ .96	+ 33%
Wisconsin	$ .92	+ 61%
Kentucky	$ .89	+ 2%
North Dakota	$ .86	+105%
Arkansas	$ .85	+ 85%
Tennessee	$ .79	+ 27%
New York	$ .79	+ 8%
Pennsylvania	$ .78	+ 70%
Mississippi	$ .74	+ 81%
Indiana	$ .74	+ 48%
Vermont	$ .70	+ 75%
West Virginia	$ .67	+ 34%
Connecticut	$ .64	+ 46%
South Dakota	$ .63	no change
South Carolina	$ .62	+ 63%
New Hampshire	$ .60	+140%
Georgia	$ .57	+ 27%
Alabama	$ .55	+ 15%
Massachusetts	$ .49	+ 40%
North Carolina	$ .47	+ 38%
Delaware	$ .45	+ 13%
Rhode Island	$ .42	*
Maine	$ .19	+ 19%

*Not available.

What Home Buyers Are Up Against

A new study shows just how expensive it has become to buy a home.

In a survey of 15 metropolitan areas by the National Association of Realtors, mortgage payments averaged $810 a month for existing homes that were sold this year. That's $428 higher than the average payment three years ago.

The findings—

	Average Home Price	Monthly Mortgage Payment*
San Francisco	$133,900	$1,403
Los Angeles	$120,100	$1,234
Washington, D.C.	$100,900	$1,048
New York	$ 93,600	$ 978
Houston	$ 95,000	$ 974
Minneapolis	$ 82,300	$ 830
Milwaukee	$ 78,200	$ 818
Chicago	$ 77,200	$ 812
Atlanta	$ 75,900	$ 767
Boston	$ 71,200	$ 734
Baltimore	$ 72,100	$ 716
Philadelphia	$ 64,000	$ 673
Detroit	$ 59,700	$ 625
St. Louis	$ 59,400	$ 605
Pittsburgh	$ 59,000	$ 601

*Principal and interest on a 30-year, 80 percent loan financed at prevailing rate; taxes and insurance not included.

lize by inflating more slowly, but prices never come down. This means that buying a house during the "low" times may seem like a temporary bargain in this inflationary world. But more importantly, since the price of housing always is at an all-time high (except for in a very few depressed areas), there will not be a better time to buy than now! During the 1970s the price of the average home in the United States rose about 150 percent, and there is no reason to expect any less of an inflation jump in home prices in the 1980s.

The purpose of showing housing trends is to acknowledge that even the low times are ideal for the creative home buyer to take the plunge. As we have seen, when homes are not selling and money is tight, sellers are more eagerly apt to listen to and negotiate with a creative buyer. In other words, real-estate lows represent a buyer's market.

Traditionally, November through February is the slowest real-estate season (a buyer's market), and peak months are May through August. The chart on the following page illustrates the fluctuation in the number of homes sold over eight years.

The number of homes being sold in any given month, however, is only a superficial representation of whether or not the housing market has become a buyer's market. There are many underlying factors, including prevailing interest rates, monies available and the individual considerations of each sale.

No matter what the month, you will find homeowners who *need* to sell but who are having trouble selling. These desperate souls will be willing to negotiate creatively. (A special tip: Always find out how long the home you are interested in has been on the market. Though other factors may be involved, if the home has been on the market for more than four months, it probably is overpriced! Know-

EXISTING SINGLE-FAMILY HOMES SOLD IN THE UNITED STATES

Date	Jan.	Feb.	Mar.	Apr.	May	Jun.	Jul.	Aug.	Sep.	Oct.	Nov.	Dec.
1975	2060000	2230000	2290000	2390000	2470000	2510000	2450000	2530000	2630000	2680000	2740000	2780000
1976	2810000	2930000	2900000	2940000	2960000	3110000	3100000	3110000	3210000	3160000	3220000	3340000
1977	3430000	3360000	3580000	3530000	3640000	3630000	3650000	3710000	3760000	3710000	3860000	3890000
1978	3900000	3830000	3970000	4090000	4000000	4040000	3990000	3960000	3930000	4000000	4150000	3980000
1979	3860000	3990000	3960000	3990000	4090000	3800000	3820000	3840000	3940000	3770000	3480000	3390000
1980	3330000	3190000	2970000	2540000	2480000	2600000	2930000	3050000	3400000	3210000	3050000	2910000
1981	2720000	2700000	2630000	2720000	2640000	2650000	2490000	2300000	2150000	2020000	1980000	2000000
1982	1890000	1990000	2030000	1960000	1920000	1980000	1910000	1860000	1910000	1990000	2150000	2260000

ing that any house will sell when it is priced right will give you an extra edge of confidence during your negotiations.)

CREATIVITY IN ACTION
Roy and Connie Todd decided to move away from the city—but not so far away that Roy wouldn't be able to keep his business appointments, which called him into the city two days a week. They chose a country community about 50 miles away, where housing costs were much lower than in the city. Although the community was rural, it was a blossoming township with a nice shopping center and the means of entertainment (a movie house, a roller-skating rink, restaurants and horseback riding) that the Todds desired. In addition, some industry was moving into the area, offering local opportunities for Roy's small but growing accounting firm. This also meant that housing prices would be going up at a fairly high annual rate.

After researching the newspapers for prices and asking many questions, the Todds spent two dreary weekends in the November rains searching for a home they'd love yet could afford. They soon decided, however, that it would be easier to work with a local real-estate agent who knew the area and could line up homes for them to see before their arrival each Saturday.

The Todds soon found the right home—for $120,000! This price was exactly $20,000 more than they had considered their upper limit, but they decided it would be worth the extra financial burden. They also knew it would take some knowledge-able and creative negotiating, as qualifying for a new loan using conventional methods was unlikely because they only had $20,000 to advance as a down payment, and Mr. Todd's net monthly income fluctuated.

Because it was November (one of the annual "buyer's market" months), they found an anxious seller. The agent recommended that the Todds extend an offer to the sellers based on these factors: (1) The first mortgage on the home was for $65,000 and *totally assumable; (2) with $20,000 as a down payment, the agent was sure the sellers would be willing to carry a second mortgage at a reasonable interest rate—and even, possibly, allow the Todds to forgo payments for the first six months. With these factors in mind, the Todds made an offer of $117,000. (It is common to offer less than the asking price.)*

Although the first mortgage was assumable, and the $20,000 would seem a reasonable down payment to most people, the sellers wanted to invest in a small horse ranch and needed all their equity in cash. The sellers' agent suggested that the Todds find a private lender for the second mortgage and then return with a new offer.

Fortunately, Connie and Roy had a quick-thinking agent who suggested a different approach. The agent pointed out that because it was November, with even slower months for real estate sales ahead, and because the sellers needed to complete their investment arrangements in the horse-ranch deal by January 15, the Todds should not bow too quickly to these demands. In other words, the sellers were desperate, so why not approach them again with the same offer? This time the buyers would suggest to the sellers that they find a second-mortgage lender. This offensive action paid off for the Todds.

The two agents, attempting to secure the deal while keeping their own clients' best interests in mind, put together the following counter-offer, which would give everyone an affordable, workable deal—the best kind of real-estate transaction:

The Todds would assume the $65,000 first mortgage and pay $20,000 down. The sellers would carry the second mortgage on a contingency basis, pending their real-estate agent's ability to sell it to a private mortgage lender before the close of escrow (the agent felt confident that he could accomplish this task). Because selling a second-mortgage loan usually requires offering a discounted price to the new lender, the Todds agreed to pay the full asking price for the house, $120,000, instead of the $117,000 they had originally offered.

Note: *Offering a discount to sell a loan is common. When selling a home-mortgage loan, you should expect the price to be discounted by 10 to 25 percent. In this particular case, the second mortgage was for $35,000, and the sellers sold it to a new lender for $29,750—a 15 percent discount. But the Todds will still owe the new lender, who now owns their second mortgage, the full $35,000. As we saw in Chapter Three, private mortgage lenders also most often take on short-term loans of three to seven years. But even with these tough terms—the discount and a short payback date—the Todds benefited by getting a reasonable interest rate that was amortized over a long period of time so that their monthly interest-only payments would be less.*

Even though the Todds simply agreed to pay the full asking price, which, given the local market, was reasonable to begin with, the arrangement was at least a psychological compromise to the sellers, who suffered the loss of the discounted second-mortgage sale.

In addition, because Connie and Roy originally had asked the sellers to waive payments on the second mortgage for six months, the sellers agreed to let the Todds pay only $15,000 down (instead of the $20,000) to help them finance their moving costs and initial loan payments. The $5,000 then became a third-mortgage loan carried by the sellers.

In summary, the Todds made a $15,000 down payment and assumed a $65,000 first-mortgage loan with monthly payments of approximately $680. A private lender carried the second mortgage for interest-only payments of approximately $400 a month, with the entire amount of principal due in five years. And, finally, the sellers carried a third mortgage of $5,000, with monthly payments of $75, which were to begin after six months. (Even if Connie and Roy had been able to qualify for a new first-mortgage loan through a conventional lender, they would have needed more than $20,000 for a down payment, and their monthly payments would have been about $250 a month higher than the total of their combined payments in fact.)

The Todds' case is an excellent illustration of how everyone can win using creative negotiating in purchasing a home.

THE PSYCHOLOGY OF APPROACHING THE SELLER

You have analyzed your financial situation, developed a plan to accomplish your home-buying goal and learned something about the financing options available to you. But how comfortable do you feel about presenting yourself to a seller? An interesting role-playing develops when seller and buyer negotiate (whether they actually meet face to face or communicate through their realtors is irrelevant). One party will take the offensive role and the other the defensive role. And who really is the underdog? Is it the person aching to buy, or the one who desperately wants to sell? The answer is up to you.

You will be able to take the offense by virtue of your confidence and your knowledge of creative financing; however, here are some extra points on how to have the upper hand when approaching the seller:

1. *Avoid falling in love with a dream house.* Buying a home is a major ordeal emotionally—especially if your income is modest and your savings are minimal. But knowing that sooner or later you will find the right house for you, and that you will be able to negotiate creatively— and successfully—should leave you feeling free to terminate any negotiation that clearly won't work given your financial situation.

2. *Conceal your enthusiasm and approach the seller apathetically.* While first viewing a home, show only modest interest. This will put you in an offensive position, allowing you to ask from a position of strength the many questions you will want answered before negotiations begin:

- How much is the seller asking?
- How long has the house been on the market?
- How long has the seller lived in the home?
- Why is the seller moving?
- Is the neighborhood noisy?
- Does the property have a septic tank, or is it attached to a sewer system? (If it has a septic tank, have there been problems with it? If so, how often?)
- Is there an assumable loan or other financing available?
- How heavy is the street traffic?
- How many square feet are there in the house?
- Where is the seller moving?

Ask these questions at random, responding to the answers with silent indifference (or even disappointment when appropriate). You already may know many of the answers if you are working with an agent, but ask anyway if you have the opportunity. It will get the sellers talking, which will help you discover their motivations and needs.

Never start negotiations on the spot. Leave, indicating that you have other homes to inspect, and thank the sellers for their time. This will put *you* in the psychological position of accepting or rejecting the home.

3. *When negotiating, show concern for the seller's needs.* Your attitude already has placed the seller in a defensive position, so be willing to compromise when necessary. As the "Creativity in Action" stories show, a buyer can change his or her approach so that the deal is more appealing to the seller without changing the actual amount of the offer. Both parties can get what they need!

By thoroughly understanding your own financial

situation, you can sway the seller. Your flexibility in negotiations stems from knowing that you won't have to qualify for a large conventional loan; but you will have to decide what size of payments you can handle each month. In the spring of 1981, the *San Francisco Chronicle* reported that 80 percent of the buyers of median-priced homes were paying 34 percent of their net income on monthly mortgage payments. This is an astounding jump from just three years earlier, when mortgage payments averaged only 22 percent of the buyer's net income.

Remember, you want to get a good deal, and the real-estate market is fast-paced. When you find a house you want, make an offer. Don't wait for a wave of certainty to envelop you. It won't happen! (But there are times when a contract can be "left open," which can buy you a few days thinking time. Read Chapter Eight, *The Contract.*)

5

WHERE TO BUY

When a new household finds its place
Among the myriad homes of earth,
It's like a new start just sprung to birth.
Longfellow, "The Hanging of the
                                    Crane," *1874*

That part of the southern and western United States known as the sunbelt experienced a decade of growth in the 1970s as millions of families headed for their place in the sun. But now, due to overpopulation, crowded highways, pollution, increased crime and (last but not least) the high cost of housing, many people are turning away from major cities, whether they are in the sunbelt or not. And, in order to attract quality personnel, industry is following these people to locales outside the main metropolitan areas.

Instead of the San Francisco Bay Area, Los Angeles or Dallas, industry is moving to places such as Scottsdale, Arizona; Raleigh, North Carolina; or Corvallis, Oregon. Communications and travel have become so advanced that it is much easier for large corporations, as well as small businesses, to prosper in these previously less developed areas. Thus the 1980s promises to be a lucrative time for home buying—for personal use, or as an investment—in rural areas, because as industry moves in, prices of homes will rise.

Also there has been a mass trend toward renovation of many rundown parts of our cities. Those people who have

61

a strong desire to live within city limits to be near cultural centers, and to avoid the rising costs of commuting from the suburbs, have started a movement giving new life to many large urban areas.

Although renovation costs for these homes can be high once the home is occupied, most work can be done by the homeowner during free time when extra money is earned. But the initial prices are far below what one might expect to pay for housing in the city. And one of the most exciting attractions for those who renovate, is the prospect of living in a home with the quality and elegance of construction typical of earlier decades.

Certain city neighborhoods develop a social reputation as renovation centers; local newspapers and magazines will mention them. Investigate these neighborhoods first, as the home values there already will be rising.

IS IT BETTER TO BE RICH IN A POOR NEIGHBORHOOD, OR POOR IN A RICH ONE?

Before considering all the investment angles of buying your home, first determine what needs and wants you seek to fulfill by owning a home. Then buying a home you will be proud of will become more important to you than buying it strictly because it is a "good buy."

For example, you may care more about being close to a park and your church than you do about being near work and transportation. But if you buy a home simply because it is a bargain, you may regret your decision. After people have bought homes in neighborhoods they really didn't care for much, the high spirits that come from owning their own home often quickly diminish; such a home usually is sold before it has become profitable or even practical to them. So here are a few property-buying hints that will bring you maximum equity (no matter how long you stay) and will help you to be happy with the home you choose.

Real-estate prices are rising almost everywhere, but some neighborhoods are known to maintain a quiet, tree-lined-street atmosphere—in these areas you can expect a higher yearly increase in equity. Sometimes the character of a neighborhood is revealed in its name or nickname; every city has a "Park View Lane" and an "Automobile Row." Where would you rather buy? The point is—it is better to buy the most run down home in a nice neighborhood and then renovate the home than to purchase the fanciest home in a less appealing neighborhood, even if the home does cost less.

Also, consider the general growth of the area. If shopping centers and offices will open there, the demand for housing in the area will rise, as will the housing prices. But even in such ideal areas, it is wise to investigate your future home's immediate surroundings. If there is a freeway easement along the back of the property, or if a chemical plant will be built down the street, you may have trouble selling the home later.

Become an expert on the area of your choice. Know how many homes are on the market there, how often and how long before they are sold. Learn the price range (for example, what size homes, with what type of features, are selling for how much). By acquiring a good feel for the real-estate market in the area, you will gain a great deal of security when you begin negotiating for the purchase of your own home. You will know when you are getting a good deal, when you are compromising, and when you are being asked to pay more for what you want.

If you are working with a real-estate agent, he or she can provide you with this comparative information. But even working on your own, it shouldn't take long to gather the facts you need. The classified section of a newspaper is the greatest single source of information on local real-estate activities. By reading ads, making a few phone calls for further information, and actually looking at homes you might be interested in buying, you will be able to compile quite a complete reference sheet.

NOTE: Real-estate firms have a form called a "comp sheet," which compares a particular home to others that are for sale, or that recently have been sold, in the same neighborhood. Agents have many sources for such statistics, from weekly real-estate-market sheets to computers. Even before seriously considering a particular home, you can gather a wealth of information on the area of your choice from a local realtor.

CREATIVITY IN ACTION

Joel and Karen Hoyt had been married for three years. They had talked about buying a house but never felt they could afford it. Then Karen found out she was to have a baby, and they would have to move from their apartment. Buying a home became their greatest desire.

The many home ads in the newspaper that Joel read included this one: "For sale by owner: 3-bedroom, 1-bath house in lovely Olive Grove area. $72,000." The ad didn't tell him much, but it seemed like a reasonable price for that section of town, which was known for being quiet and was occupied mostly by older folks. Also, it was near Joel's work, which meant he would not have to commute.

Driving into the neighborhood, the Hoyts noticed a for-sale sign in front of the smallest, worst-kept house on the street— explaining the reasonable price. But the house had character, and all the other homes on the street were well taken care of.

The sellers were young and never had lived in the house; they had rented it for the four and one-half years since they had purchased it. After speaking with the sellers, Mr. and Mrs. Cunningham, Joel and Karen learned that the first-mortgage balance on the home was $35,000 and assumable. They knew *they'd have no trouble assuming that loan, but the other $37,000 would be a problem to them unless the Cunninghams would carry the second mortgage.*

The Cunninghams, however, refused to carry the second mortgage. They had opened escrow on a new home, and their $37,000 equity was needed. And $72,000 was their firm selling price (even though they would not be contracting a real-estate agent, which would save them agent commission fees).

Joel and Karen had no idea how to continue negotiations, so they left to phone a real-estate agent friend, who had offered to help them. Kurt, the agent, said he knew of the house and that it had been in the papers periodically for about two months. Combining the knowledge Kurt already had about the house with what Joel had told him about the Cunninghams' purchase of a new home gave Kurt an idea.

Although the final details of the offer were foreign to Joel and Karen, the offer that Kurt put together was quite simple:

Offer the full asking price of $72,000 with a $5,000 down payment, and the sellers would carry a "wrap-around" of $67,000. In other words a second mortgage to be carried by the seller for $27,000 would be "wrapped" with the first-mortgage loan of $35,000, so that Joel and Karen would be making one loan payment to the Cunninghams to cover the payment of both loans (as the Cunninghams would continue making the bank payments on the existing first loan). The payment made by Joel and Karen to the sellers then would be on a $67,000 short-term loan, amortized over a 30-year period, at 14 percent interest, with the balance due in six years. The Hoyts' payments, including property taxes (which were figured into the first-mortgage loan), would be about $845 a month.

Prior to making this offer, Kurt, Joel and Karen calculated exactly what terms would produce an affordable monthly payment for the Hoyts. An $845 monthly house payment, on one salary, would require some sacrifices, but the Hoyts knew they could do it.

The sellers' real incentive to accept this offer was the substantial interest payments they would be receiving: because the loan is a wrap-around (as discussed in the Creative Financing Section of Chapter Three), they would be keeping the bonus difference between the interest rate they owed on the first mortgage, and the rate the Hoyts would be paying on the entire wrapped loan. In this case, about $355 a month was owed on the first mortgage; the Cunninghams' bonus in interest from that loan was about $100 a month; and the interest-only payments they would receive on the second mortgage was $385 a month. They also would be able to use the $5,000 down payment to help them get into their new home; and, most of all, they were now relieved of the pressure to sell before escrow on their new home closed. Finally there also were tax benefits for these sellers in not receiving their entire equity in cash before they were ready to reinvest.

What the offer meant to the Hoyts was that they could move into a home they could afford without having to qualify for a new loan. The home was in an area in which they wanted to live, and the home was purchased at an interest rate below currently prevailing rates, and for a minimal down payment. In six years they would be able to assume the existing first loan and refinance the second, or refinance the entire loan—whichever would bring them lower payments at that time.

The contract was agreed upon and three weeks later Joel and Karen toasted with champagne and shared their first dinner sitting on the living-room floor of their new home.

FINDING A BARGAIN HOME

Bargain homes can be found in any city, town or neighborhood, because getting a bargain simply means paying less than the market value in that area. What actually is a bargain depends on you, your income and what price you pay for a home in a neighborhood in which you want to live. When searching newspaper ads for a bargain home, try to avoid answering ads that do not list a price, as this often is a waste of time and usually no bargain. Also, most real-estate firms do not include addresses in their advertisements so that you have to phone them for information. This is understandable, since the agent is expected to screen prospective buyers so that a seller does not have lookers who may be simply curious knocking at all hours. However, if you decide not to work through an agent but wish to see a particular home, an agent will often give you the address of the home if you say you only want to *drive by* to see it, then take the agent's name and indicate you will call back if you are still interested. If the agent refuses to give you the address, and you really want to know where the home is, offer to meet the agent there to preview the home with you. But *do not* feel any obligation to this agent beyond this one meeting simply because he or she happened to answer the phone. You may establish an immediate, lucky rapport with the agent and want him or her to begin representing you. But don't let yourself be intimidated into using his or her services. (Read Chapter Seven, "The Pros and Cons of Real-estate Agents.")

You may have heard that bargain homes are those sold directly by the owners, with no agents involved. Why? Because then you, the buyer, won't have to pay a real-estate agent's commission. This is not true. The advantage for a seller to sell the home without an agent is that the *seller* won't have to pay an agent's commission. In other words, the seller still might ask the same price as the family next door, who is selling with the commissioned help of an agent. The seller pays the agent! A seller's working without an agent is only advantageous to the buyer (1) when the seller substantially lowers the home's price below market value (about 6 percent) to make up for the agent's commission, because the seller wants a quick sale; or (2) when you, the buyer, can successfully ask the seller to split the equivalent of an agent's commission with you by lowering the price at least 3 percent. Only in these ways can you create a bargain when purchasing a for-sale-by-owner home.

When searching the newspaper ads, or talking to sellers, look for the following key words; they indicate whether the seller is motivated to bargain creatively.

- Will consider trade
- Job relocation
- Must move
- Property needs improvements
- Divorce
- Death, family liquidating
- Will carry financing
- Retiring
- New home in escrow

These are bargain situations. But no matter who you negotiate with, your ability to negotiate creatively will make the purchase an actual bargain. Know your options thoroughly, or work with an agent you trust as a quick thinker and who is well informed in creative financing. Most importantly, when you find a bargain, be prepared to make an offer, because a bargain in real estate moves fast!

(Here's an additional idea: Turn your home into a bargain *after* you have moved in, by adding on to it and doing your own construction. Buying a small home and adding rooms—are even renting one or two extra rooms—is becoming common.)

BUYING INVESTMENT PROPERTY

The decision to buy any property takes all the motivation and courage that most people can muster. And if you live in an area where housing is particularly expensive, and buying a first home seems beyond your preconceived financial limit, then buying a second property as an investment is not even a topic for consideration.

But wait. Buying rental property may provide the initial credit/financial boost you need before buying your first home or it may become a way to expand your investment portfolio after buying your first home. Using the creative financing techniques found throughout this book, it is possible to buy property with little or no money down. And taking into account that there still are places in the United States where housing prices are low enough for rental fees to nearly cover mortgage payments, buying income property can be very profitable, not to mention the tax benefits of owning rental property.

If you decide to buy income property outside your area, look first at a rural area that appeals to you. Knowing that you own property in an inviting community not only builds your confidence in owning, but also can give you security in our unpredictable economy. And all the while you will own a home that could possibly be paying for itself and growing in equity at the same time.

If the property you choose is too far away for you to manage personally, you may be able to hire a local property manager (often these are real-estate agents) who will take care of the home for a minimal fee. The fee usually is 10 percent of the monthly rent. You can best find a property manager by inquiring at real-estate offices in that area.

You may have even greater real-estate ambitions and look forward to buying lots of investment properties—and believe you can do it! In that case, read Robert G. Allen's book *Nothing Down*, (Simon and Schuster, 1980). It offers attitudes and concepts for becoming wealthy through ownership of income property. And, like everything else you decide you really want to do, it is possible!

CREATIVITY IN ACTION

Robert G. Allen, a successful real-estate investor, bragged of being able to walk into any city with only $100 in his pocket for living expenses and buy an excellent piece of real estate within 72 hours. In January 1981, his challenge was accepted. The city he had to conquer had one of the three toughest real estate markets in the United States—San Francisco.

Allen's approach to finding a piece of property for nothing down was to find a desperate seller who no longer wanted his or her real estate. During the negotiations, Allen would need to show the seller that both buyer and seller can win by accepting Allen's no-down-payment offer.

The result. *Within 24 hours, Allen had bought a $158,000 condominium in San Francisco's exclusive Diamond Heights area, with no down payment!*

The method. *Allen would assume an existing first mortgage of $125,000. The seller would carry a second-mortgage loan for $21,000, and a third mortgage for $12,000. Both the second- and third-mortgage loans would require interest-only payments, at 10 percent, with the balance due in three years.*

The seller had decided to carry both a second- and a third-mortgage loan with the intention of selling the second, for $21,000, to another investor for cash. Because it would be easier to sell the $21,000 second mortgage if Allen were to show some financial credibility by making a sizable down payment, the contract was written with a purchase price of $173,000, rather than the actual price of $158,000. Then, in a separate addendum to the contract, a $15,000 credit was given to Allen for home *improvements. Thus, if the purchaser of the $21,000 second mortgage looked only at the original contract, it would appear to him or her that Allen had made a $15,000 down payment.*

This type of transaction could easily work for a buyer intending to live in the home, but how did Allen, only an investor, plan to handle the monthly payments? He would place an advertisement offering half ownership in the home if the tenant simply would make all payments. Also, this tenant would have the option to buy Allen out for a flat $6,000 in the first year. A fantastic deal for the tenant and Robert Allen. The worst Allen could do in this transaction would be to make $6,000 in 24 hours!

6

THE DOLLARS AND SENSE OF BUYING A HOME

The greatest financial risk today can be in playing it safe. With the type of economy that has developed in the United States, it is not uncommon to see inflation outdoing the interest rates of conventional modes of investment; after years of saving, we can end up with less than we started with!

Without realizing it, most Americans have been throwing in the towel on a secure financial future for themselves. By depending on their savings accounts, Social Security payments and minimal pension income to carry them through the retirement years, they may be committing financial suicide.

There are many ways to invest extra earnings; each has its own degree of risk. Investment in real estate, however, still is known as the lowest-risk hedge against inflation.

Note the following examples comparing real estate as an investment with other forms of investment (there is an often overlooked but important point made here):

STOCKS: You buy 400 shares at $50 a share. The total investment is $20,000. In three years you sell the 400 shares for $75 a share. Your profit is $10,000. You have made a 50 percent profit on your original investment. (The stock market has a history of callousness and usually is profitable only to the expert investor who spends a great deal of time following it.)

DIAMONDS: You purchase eight quality-cut stones for $2,500 each. Your total investment is $20,000. In three years you sell the eight stones for $5,712 each (a well-timed diamond investment can earn as much as 30 percent annually averaged over a number of years). Your profit is $25,696. You have made a 128 percent profit on your original investment. (The diamond world is controlled by one corporation, which has ensured diamond prices never deflate. However, it is necessary to invest for a *minimum* of three years for such a profit, as yearly activity is unpredictable.)

TREASURY BILLS: You secure four $5,000 Treasury bills. The total investment is $20,000. (At present it is possible to buy Treasury bills for a maximum of one year only in minimal increments of $5,000. But for the sake of continuity here, let's say you rebought every year for three years, using your original investment *plus* the interest you had accumulated.) After three years, your profit is $7,800 (at a very generous interest rate of 12 percent). You have made a profit of 39 percent on your original investment.

REAL ESTATE: You buy a $100,000 home. Your total investment is a $20,000 down payment. In three years housing prices have gone up a conservative 12 percent annually; you sell for $140,492. Your profit is $40,492. You have made a 203 percent profit on your original investment.

Do you get the point? In real estate you make a profit on

the entire worth of the home, even though you have invested only a portion of that worth.

It is true that over the three-year period you would be making monthly loan payments, which could be considered an additional sum of money added to your original invested (down payment) amount. However, these monthly loan payments are, for the most part, interest payments, which are completely deductible on your federal income-tax returns. Also, consider that other potential home buyers who invested in stocks, diamonds or Treasury bills instead of real estate also are paying housing costs without having the benefits that you reap as a homeowner.

Whether you are considering a first or second home, dollar for dollar, real estate seems to be the best low-risk hedge against inflation. Make the extra effort to own property—when it comes to securing your future, it's worth it!

NOTE: Even though investment in real estate may continually bring particularly high returns, it is smart to be a well-rounded investor in an unstable economy. So *after* you have bought at least your first home, if you have money to begin an investment portfolio, consult a qualified investment counselor.

CREATIVITY IN ACTION

Lisa Goodman and Sarah Thomas worked for the same insurance company, and they had become good friends, both enjoying the single life. Lisa was promoted to be manager of personnel a year ago, and Sarah was an executive secretary for the vice president of the company.

One day at lunch Sarah complained about yet another rental increase for her apartment. Feeling the new rent was much too high for the quality of the complex, she had decided to move.

Lisa, who also lived alone, said that she, too, would like to move to a nicer place. As they talked, they recognized that they might afford a nicer apartment by moving in together and splitting the costs. But it wasn't until someone else at the table suggested that they buy, instead of rent, that the conversation turned to condominiums.

Lisa and Sarah discussed three different condominium complexes they knew of, and one in particular that was relatively new; it had all the extras such as tennis courts, a swimming pool, and a health spa. In these first few moments of enthusiasm, the women decided to inspect the condominiums the following Saturday to see what was available.

The condominiums were lovely. Even though they were only a year old, there already were three or four units for resale. One of those resale units was holding an "open house" that day. The girls went into the open unit and found two large bedrooms, a living room with a cathedral ceiling and a fireplace, a separate dining area—and a real-estate agent. Lisa and Sarah liked the agent. She was not the agent contracted by the sellers, but she was from the same office. This agent was simply holding the open house as a favor for a coworker, so knowing that this agent was not the seller's representative, the women sat down to talk financing with her.

The asking price for the condominium was $94,500; there was an assumable, variable-interest-rate loan at 13.5 percent for $61,000; the sellers would carry a second-mortgage loan for $20,000 at 13 percent, with interest-only payments for three years; and the sellers wanted the remaining $13,500 in cash as a down payment. The agent assured them the condominium was fairly priced and that the terms were excellent. Also, this was the first weekend the condominium had been listed for resale, and she didn't expect it to stay available for more than a few days.

Feeling a certain amount of anxiety and enthusiasm, Lisa and Sarah drove to a nearby restaurant to discuss the situation. The conversation was made easier by virtue of Lisa's past experience.

She had had a boyfriend who was a real-estate agent, and she had learned quite a bit about real estate from him.

First, Lisa and Sarah agreed the condominium would sell soon, so the question was, did they really want to buy it? Yes.

But could they meet the financial terms? Assuming the $61,000 loan would mean payments of about $700 a month, and the interest-only payments on the $20,000 second loan would be about $215 a month, for a monthly total of $915. Adding property taxes and insurance payments, they estimated that each month's payments would be about $1,000, or $500 each. Recognizing this brought a wave of excitement to them both. Sarah already was spending $350 a month on rent, not including the announced $35 monthly increase, and Lisa was paying $375 a month for rent. Since their payments would be going into the equity on their home—and not "wasted" as rent—the extra expense for the condominium seemed more than worth it.

Their last consideration was the down payment. They had been told it would be $13,500, plus an estimated $1,500 in closing costs. (Lisa really felt they should go in with a full offer of $94,500 so that they didn't chance having their offer rejected.) So $15,000 in cash was needed, or $7,500 each. Could they advance this amount of money?

Lisa knew she could; she had $4,000 in a savings account, at least $2,500 in stocks that had been a gift years ago, and the rest she could get by selling an old car that had been sitting around since she bought her new one.

Sarah was a little more concerned. She had $1,200 in savings; she could borrow $1,500 using a Visa card if she had to; and since Lisa had a stereo set they could share, Sarah could sell hers, along with a seldom-played guitar, for $1,000. This totaled $3,700; but another $3,800 was needed. Although Sarah never had asked her family for money before, she felt they might be willing to help out under the circumstances. So she decided she would ask her dad and her grandmother to split the amount she needed, with the stipulation that she would pay them back in *three years (when Lisa and Sarah had to refinance the second-mortgage loan).*

Speculating that Sarah's relatives would loan her the money, Sara and Lisa made the needed quick decision. They returned to the condominium and had the agent present the sellers with an offer. It was accepted that evening.

Sarah's father loaned his daughter $5,000 (the $3,800 she needed plus an extra $1,200 to make the move easier), but with the wise advice that both women see a real-estate lawyer and have a separate contract written up that would specifically outline their obligations to each other as cobuyers. (See the discussion of cobuyers in Chapter Three.) Sarah and Lisa moved in 45 days later.

Before you begin negotiating the purchase of your home, obviously you need to know exactly what monthly payments you can afford. What size loan, and at what interest rate, will reach that monthly limit? Most stationery stores sell small booklets with computed and charted loan-payment schedules. The charts are based on loans fully amortized from one to 40 years, using simple-interest rates ranging from 10 percent to 20 percent, and loan amounts from $25 to $100,000. The booklets are comprehensive and an ideal tool for instant calculation. Ask for a booklet containing mortgage payment tables. The tables opposite are samples from such a booklet.

INTEREST RATES
Always obtain the lowest possible interest rate amortized over the longest period of time available. Of course, this may seem to be common sense, but note this example of the significance it will have on your monthly payments: on a $50,000 loan at 11 percent interest, amortized over a 25-year period, your monthly payments would be $490; for

13¼%   Monthly Payment

TERM AMOUNT $	19 YEARS	20 YEARS	21 YEARS	22 YEARS	23 YEARS	24 YEARS	25 YEARS
25	31	30	30	30	30	29	29
50	61	60	59	59	59	58	58
75	91	90	89	88	88	87	87
100	1.21	1.19	1.18	1.18	1.17	1.16	1.15
200	2.41	2.38	2.36	2.34	2.33	2.32	2.30
300	3.61	3.57	3.54	3.51	3.49	3.46	3.45
400	4.82	4.76	4.72	4.68	4.65	4.62	4.59
500	6.02	5.95	5.90	5.85	5.81	5.77	5.74
600	7.22	7.14	7.08	7.02	6.97	6.93	6.89
700	8.42	8.33	8.25	8.18	8.13	8.08	8.03
800	9.63	9.52	9.43	9.35	9.29	9.23	9.18
900	10.83	10.71	10.61	10.52	10.45	10.38	10.33
1000	12.03	11.90	11.79	11.69	11.61	11.53	11.47
2000	24.06	23.79	23.57	23.38	23.21	23.06	22.94
3000	36.09	35.69	35.36	35.06	34.81	34.59	34.41
4000	48.11	47.58	47.13	46.75	46.41	46.12	45.87
5000	60.13	59.48	58.91	58.43	58.01	57.65	57.34
6000	72.16	71.37	70.70	70.12	69.62	69.18	68.81
7000	84.18	83.27	82.48	81.80	81.22	80.71	80.27
8000	96.21	95.16	94.26	93.49	92.82	92.24	91.74
9000	108.23	107.05	106.03	105.18	104.42	103.77	103.21
10000	120.26	118.95	117.82	116.86	116.02	115.30	114.68
11000	132.28	130.84	129.61	128.54	127.62	126.83	126.14
12000	144.31	142.74	141.39	140.23	139.23	138.36	137.61
13000	156.33	154.63	153.17	151.91	150.83	149.89	149.08
14000	168.36	166.53	164.96	163.60	162.43	161.42	160.54
15000	180.38	178.42	176.75	175.28	174.03	172.95	172.01
16000	192.41	190.31	188.52	186.97	185.63	184.48	183.48
17000	204.43	202.21	200.31	198.65	197.24	196.01	194.94
18000	216.46	214.10	212.09	210.34	208.84	207.54	206.41
19000	228.48	226.00	223.88	222.03	220.44	219.07	217.88
20000	240.51	237.89	235.66	233.71	232.04	230.60	229.34
21000	252.53	249.79	247.45	245.40	243.64	242.13	240.81
22000	264.56	261.68	259.23	257.08	255.24	253.66	252.28
23000	276.58	273.58	271.02	268.77	266.85	265.19	263.75
24000	288.61	285.47	282.80	280.45	278.45	276.71	275.21
25000	300.63	297.36	294.59	292.14	290.05	288.24	286.68
26000	312.66	309.26	306.34	303.82	301.65	299.77	298.15
27000	324.68	321.15	318.12	315.51	313.25	311.30	309.61
28000	336.71	333.05	329.91	327.20	324.86	322.83	321.08
29000	348.73	344.94	341.69	338.88	336.46	334.36	332.55
30000	360.76	356.83	353.48	350.56	348.06	345.89	344.02
31000	372.78	368.73	365.25	362.25	359.66	357.42	355.48
32000	384.81	380.62	377.03	373.93	371.26	368.95	366.95
33000	396.83	392.52	388.82	385.62	382.86	380.48	378.42
34000	408.86	404.41	400.59	397.30	394.47	392.01	389.88
35000	420.88	416.31	412.37	408.99	406.07	403.54	401.35
40000	481.01	475.78	471.28	467.42	464.08	461.19	458.69
45000	541.13	535.25	530.19	525.84	522.08	518.84	516.02
50000	601.26	594.72	589.10	584.27	580.09	576.48	573.36
55000	661.39	654.19	648.01	642.69	638.10	634.13	630.69
60000	721.51	713.66	706.92	701.12	696.11	691.78	688.03
65000	781.64	773.13	765.83	759.55	754.12	749.43	745.36
70000	841.76	832.61	824.74	817.97	812.13	807.07	802.70
75000	901.89	892.08	883.65	876.40	870.14	864.72	860.03
80000	962.01	951.55	942.55	934.83	928.15	922.37	917.37
85000	1022.14	1011.02	1001.46	993.25	986.16	980.01	974.70
90000	1082.26	1070.49	1060.37	1051.68	1044.17	1037.66	1032.04
95000	1142.39	1129.96	1119.28	1110.11	1102.18	1095.31	1089.37
100000	1202.51	1189.44	1178.20	1168.53	1160.18	1152.96	1146.71

13¾%   Monthly Payment

TERM AMOUNT $	26 YEARS	27 YEARS	28 YEARS	29 YEARS	30 YEARS	35 YEARS	40 YEARS
25	29	29	29	29	29	28	28
50	57	57	57	57	57	56	56
75	86	86	85	85	85	84	84
100	1.15	1.14	1.14	1.13	1.13	1.11	1.10
200	2.29	2.28	2.27	2.26	2.26	2.23	2.20
300	3.43	3.41	3.40	3.39	3.38	3.35	3.33
400	4.57	4.55	4.53	4.52	4.51	4.47	4.44
500	5.71	5.69	5.67	5.65	5.63	5.58	5.55
600	6.85	6.82	6.80	6.78	6.76	6.70	6.66
700	7.99	7.96	7.93	7.91	7.88	7.81	7.77
800	9.14	9.10	9.06	9.04	9.01	8.93	8.88
900	10.28	10.23	10.20	10.16	10.14	10.04	9.99
1000	11.42	11.37	11.33	11.29	11.26	11.16	11.10
2000	22.83	22.74	22.65	22.58	22.52	22.31	22.20
3000	34.24	34.11	33.97	33.86	33.78	33.46	33.30
4000	45.66	45.47	45.30	45.15	45.04	44.61	44.40
5000	57.07	56.84	56.63	56.45	56.29	55.77	55.50
6000	68.48	68.20	67.95	67.74	67.55	66.92	66.60
7000	79.89	79.56	79.28	79.03	78.81	78.07	77.70
8000	91.31	90.93	90.60	90.31	90.06	89.22	88.80
9000	102.72	102.30	101.93	101.60	101.31	100.38	99.89
10000	114.13	113.66	113.25	112.89	112.58	111.53	110.99
11000	125.54	125.03	124.58	124.18	123.84	122.68	122.09
12000	136.96	136.39	135.90	135.47	135.10	133.83	133.19
13000	148.37	147.76	147.22	146.76	146.36	144.99	144.29
14000	159.78	159.12	158.55	158.05	157.63	156.14	155.39
15000	171.20	170.49	169.87	169.34	168.87	167.29	166.49
16000	182.61	181.85	181.20	180.63	180.13	178.44	177.58
17000	194.02	193.22	192.52	191.92	191.39	189.60	188.68
18000	205.43	204.59	203.85	203.20	202.64	200.75	199.78
19000	216.85	215.95	215.17	214.49	213.90	211.90	210.88
20000	228.26	227.32	226.50	225.79	225.16	223.06	221.98
21000	239.67	238.68	237.82	237.07	236.42	234.21	233.08
22000	251.08	250.05	249.15	248.36	247.68	245.36	244.18
23000	262.50	261.41	260.47	259.65	258.93	256.52	255.28
24000	273.91	272.78	271.79	270.94	270.19	267.67	266.37
25000	285.32	284.14	283.12	282.23	281.45	278.82	277.47
26000	296.74	295.51	294.44	293.52	292.71	289.97	288.57
27000	308.15	306.87	305.77	304.81	303.97	301.13	299.67
28000	319.56	318.24	317.09	316.09	315.22	312.28	310.77
29000	330.97	329.61	328.42	327.38	326.48	323.43	321.87
30000	342.39	340.97	339.74	338.67	337.74	334.58	332.97
31000	353.80	352.34	351.07	349.96	348.99	345.73	344.06
32000	365.21	363.70	362.39	361.25	360.25	356.88	355.16
33000	376.62	375.07	373.72	372.54	371.51	368.03	366.26
34000	388.04	386.43	385.04	383.83	382.77	379.19	377.36
35000	399.45	397.80	396.36	395.11	394.03	390.34	388.46
40000	456.51	454.63	452.99	451.56	450.31	446.10	443.95
45000	513.58	511.46	509.61	508.00	506.60	501.86	499.45
50000	570.64	568.28	566.23	564.45	562.90	557.63	554.94
55000	627.70	625.11	622.84	620.89	619.18	613.39	610.43
60000	684.77	681.94	679.48	677.34	675.47	669.15	665.93
65000	741.83	738.77	736.10	733.70	731.76	724.91	721.42
70000	798.90	795.60	792.72	790.22	788.05	780.67	776.91
75000	855.96	852.42	849.35	846.67	844.34	836.44	832.41
80000	913.02	909.25	905.97	903.11	900.62	892.20	887.90
85000	970.09	966.08	962.59	959.56	956.91	947.96	943.39
90000	1027.15	1022.91	1019.21	1016.00	1013.19	1003.72	998.89
95000	1084.22	1079.74	1075.84	1072.45	1069.48	1059.48	1054.38
100000	1141.28	1136.56	1132.46	1128.89	1125.78	1115.25	1109.87

the same $50,000 loan at 16 percent interest amortized over a 15-year period, your payments would be $735 a month. This difference could be critical in your decision to purchase a particular home. (If interest rates are exceptionally high, even during a "buyer's market," the market can turn into "nobody's market.")

For most real-estate loans, monthly payments are computed using the simple-interest-rate method. It is not easy to compute the amount of your payments using the simple-interest method, because the amount of interest is based on the unpaid balance of the loan's principal at the end of each pay period. And considering each pay period usually is one month, projecting monthly payments, for example, for a 25-year loan, would be more easily accomplished using a computer. This is why the mortgage-payment booklets are so useful.

In the late 1970s inflation and loan-interest rates entered an era of unpredictable change, so lenders began to redesign their loan packages to keep pace with that unpredictability. Fixed-interest rates, which have been traditional, are becoming obsolete. The following is a look at today's loan options—with one possibly to become a future favorite. NOTE: using the simple-interest-rate method, one computes how much the interest will be on the unpaid principal with each payment; but there are several ways in which a lender can design payment of the loan.

A *fixed-interest rate* means that the interest percentage you pay on your loan will remain the same for the life of the loan. All short-term loans are likely to have a fixed rate, but long-term loans (especially those of 15 years or longer) at a fixed rate are becoming increasingly hard to find. Conventional lending institutions (for example, banks and savings and loan companies) no longer are inclined to package fixed-interest-rate loans because under recent legal rulings, a new buyer may assume an existing home loan without change in the interest-rate terms of that loan. These lenders are losing money if old loans, which have been assumed, are at an interest rate lower than the current rate of inflation. Lenders would like to avoid this. So by using one of the following three methods, even if the loan is assumed by a new buyer, the interest rate will not be fixed and presumably outdated.

Variable-interest rates are controlled by government rules that allow a lender to increase the interest rate of an established loan periodically to keep pace with the prevailing market rate. The guidelines for raising rates are strict, which can benefit the borrower, or be to his or her disadvantage, depending upon the economy. The benefit is that lenders are allowed to raise rates only .5 percent in any given year, with a maximum rate increase of 2.5 percent over the entire life of the loan. The disadvantage to the borrower would come in a stable and booming economy. Suppose prevailing interest rates dropped and remained stable at a percentage less than what you are paying on your variable-interest loan, your rate would not go down to reflect the new rate. If you take on a variable-interest-rate loan, be sure there is no prepayment penalty. However if this situation does occur, an option would be to prepay the loan and refinance your home through another lender at a lower rate.

A renegotiable-rate mortgage (RRM) involves short-term renewals on a long-term mortgage loan. Say your home loan is for a 30-year period (the maximum length of a RRM loan). At predetermined intervals—every three to five years—the borrower will have to renew the loan regarding the interest rate only. This differs from short-term loans; with the RRM the borrower need not requalify for the loan, nor may any portion of the loan, except the interest rate, be changed. And the lender cannot restrict the borrower's right to renew the loan for any reason (although the borrower has the option to refinance elsewhere should interest rates be better there).

Using the RRM method, the borrower can also benefit from downward shifts in the economy. Interest rates for RRM are determined by the Federal Home Loan Bank Board; the rate represents the average of conventional home-mortgage loan rates written in any given month. However, the rates cannot decrease or increase more than .5 percent per year (if you have a four-year renewal period you could see a maximum interest-rate change of 2 percent in either direction). Over the entire life of the loan, the interest rate may not decrease or increase by more than 5 percent. Another advantage to the borrower is that no prepayment charge can be exercised after the first renewal period.

The adjustable-rate mortgage (ARM) has been established for federally chartered savings and loan companies and gives them virtually unlimited power to vary the interest rates on your loan at any time, in either direction, and for however many percentage points that they deem necessary to keep pace with prevailing rates. These shifts in your loan's rate, may or may not be reflected in the amount you must pay for any given month; as with variable-interest-rate and the RRM methods, the difference can be added on at the end of your loan period, either in monies owed or in the length of time payments are to be made.

Although lenders are not limited in the interest rates they may charge using ARM, consumer awareness will probably keep these rates within reasonable bounds as use of various loan options increases competition among lenders. Also, as each loan package is written, it is possible to establish a limit on how much the rate can vary—for instance, no more than a 3 percent to 5 percent variance over the life of that particular loan—although the lender is not mandated to include such terms.

GRADUATED PAYMENTS

Using graduated payments, a loan is computed so that the initial payments are less than they would be for a conventional loan, and thereby easier for the new home-buyer. A conventional loan is fully amortized over a long period of time—say, 15 to 40 years—with every monthly payment equal for that entire time. But when using the graduated-payment method, monthly-payment totals will begin lower and end higher than on a standard amortized payment schedule.

Graduated payments are particularly advantageous to a buyer who expects career advancements, such as a doctor who is just starting practice—he or she can afford only minimal payments now, but expects to be earning more in a few years. (It will take approximately five to seven years for your payments to reach the level where they would have begun with a conventional loan.) Initial payments can be substantially lower than they would be using other methods, so if you feel that the graduated payment method would benefit you, ask your lender, or agent, about acquiring a graduated payment loan. (Graduated-payment loans most commonly are associated with FHA loans.)

SHORT-TERM LOANS AND BALLOON PAYMENTS

Balloon payments are most often the end result of a short-term loan. The borrower's monthly payments may reflect the payments on a loan amortized for 10 to 40 years, but the actual life of a short-term loan usually will be from three to seven years. After this short period, the borrower will owe the entire unpaid balance in one large payment—known as a balloon payment. This short-term-loan approach, using balloon payments, is becoming very popular with lenders, and usually is the method used with second and third mortgages. Even large conventional lenders are beginning to offer first-mortgage, short-term loans to today's home buyers.

To the borrower, a short-term loan with a balloon payment simply means that the loan will have to be refinanced, or the home sold, to make the final principal payment at the end of the loan's term. As was mentioned earlier in the book, it is absolutely necessary for a buyer to avoid a short-term loan of less than three years; if your loan comes due and you do not have a substantial amount of equity built up—and especially if interest rates are high—you may have trouble qualifying for a refinance loan and thus may be forced to sell your home.

COMPOUND INTEREST

Compound interest is illegal in real-estate financing, although it is used occasionally. If you are acquiring a second or a third mortgage, pay attention to how the interest for the loan is computed. Unlike simple interest, compound interest is calculated by adding the unpaid interest to the principal amount of the loan and then computing the interest owed. Here is an example:

The buyer wants to borrow $20,000 for five years with interest-only payments. At a 10 percent annual interest rate, the borrower would pay about $165 a month, or $2,000 a year. Then, in five years, a balloon payment of $20,000 would be due. However, this buyer wants payments deferred for the first year and to be allowed to pay that year's interest at the end of the loan period, along with the entire principal balance. The proper (simple-interest method) way to handle this loan would be to make the $2,000-a-year payments (in monthly increments) during years two through five, and after five years the $20,000 principal plus the first year's interest would be due; this would equal $22,000.

The illegal (compound-interest method) way to handle computation of this loan would be to take the first year's unpaid interest and add it to the $20,000, totaling $22,000, then calculate the 10 percent interest which is to be paid in years two through five. Annual interest payments have just jumped to $2,200, or a monthly payment of approximately $183. In the end you have paid an extra $800. Beware! This can unintentionally be figured by an agent or private lender. Pay attention to the financing process of your payment schedule.

CREATIVITY IN ACTION

Three years ago Carla Simmons was divorced. She left the marriage with about $28,000 from the sale of their home, a few stocks and a small monthly alimony. At the time of the divorce Carla had been unemployed for several years; she felt this would keep her from qualifying for a new home loan. But she really wanted a place of her own—just some place small until she could decide what she wanted to do next in life.

In the hills above town, there was a small house that had been for sale for quite some time. It was a vacant, 800-square-foot house, on a fair-sized lot that had been left to nature and was now all weeds. The house was too small for and generally undesirable to most people, so in the pinch of not being able to sell, the owner/seller had changed his for-sale ad in the newspaper, to an ad for a lease/purchase option.

It was an ideal opportunity for Carla. Financially, the lease/purchase option meant a $2,500 deposit, and monthly payments to the owner that would cover the existing mortgage payments, which were about $445 a month. The purchase option of the contract would have to be exercised within three years for her to take advantage of the current fixed $80,500 purchase price. This certainly seemed reasonable to Carla, so she signed the papers and moved in.

Three years later, Carla loved the home. With a renewed enthusiasm for life, she had made many home improvements: She had landscaped the property, with a garden; she had painted and papered walls; and she had added new light fixtures and curtains—all at her own expense. She wanted to buy the house.

Carla felt comfortable trying to buy now because she had gone back to work at a travel agency—in her old profession—and was doing well. She approached the owner of the home to discuss the terms of its purchase. The owner became extremely upset. He knew the home's market value had gone up $30,000 from the fixed $80,500 price he had offered Carla under the lease/purchase option, and he had hoped the due date for her option would slip by without her acting on it. But Carla's contract with him for the home was well-written, and he had no legal recourse but to allow her to buy the home at $80,500. His revenge was to make it difficult for Carla: he demanded all equity in cash.

The original loan, with a balance of $36,000, was assumable at 12 percent interest. This was good news to Carla, but now she needed $42,000 in cash. (Carla needed only $42,000 because she already had paid $2,500 down when she moved in.) She still had $22,000 saved from her divorce, but with current high-interest rates, she was afraid she wouldn't qualify, on her income, for a short-term second-mortgage loan of $20,000. Carla spent two weeks researching possibilities for new loans and for second mortgages through the hard-money lenders. In every case the high interest rates were too high for her.

Through a real-estate agent who had given her leads on mortgage lenders, Carla heard of a local alternative lending company that worked with investors who contributed down-payment monies to share the home's equity. Through this company she found an investor who supplemented her $22,000 in cash by investing the additional $20,000 needed for the down payment. The investor's name would go on the deed as a cobuyer, and in four years, his original investment of $20,000 would be returned to him, plus 50 percent of the home's equity developed

To the investor this would mean a 100 percent return on his investment (or 25 percent a year, as he would be making an equity profit on the entire worth of the home and not just his invested portion). To Carla it meant buying a home at a price $30,000 below market value, with no increase in her current monthly payments (during the four years, Carla would not have to make payments to the investor on the borrowed $20,000). After four years the home would be appraised at approximately $142,000. Carla still would owe about $33,000 on the first loan and about $41,000 to her investor—a total of $74,000. Carla could easily refinance, based on her equity at that time, but refinancing (after a period of four years) would bring her payments up to about $1,000 a month. Thus, instead of using an investor, it might have been wiser for Carla to take the higher payments to begin with, by financing the entire amount owed on the home (the $36,000 assumable first mortgage and the $20,000 acquired from the investor) for one new, long-term loan. A new long-term loan would have meant no more headaches or fee expenses for refinancing another short-term loan. But Carla could not afford the monthly payments, and bringing in an investor who didn't require monthly payments was the only way for her to keep the house. So after four years, Carla again will face the problem of not being able to afford the monthly payments. She will either have to sell the house (in which case she would have about $70,000 clear equity to buy again), bring in a roommate to help with expenses, or refinance for more than she needs and thus use some of her equity to help with the monthly payments. Carla foresaw these future options, and in any case, she was delighted to keep her home and have, at least for another four years, the growing equity and/or the time to work out a solution.

The papers were signed and the tranaction completed 15 days prior to the expiration date of the lease/purchase option. Once again Carla was a homeowner, establishing some financial security for the future.

7

THE PROS AND CONS OF REAL ESTATE AGENTS

*No one is so rich that he does not
need another's help; and
no one is so poor that he cannot
ask assistance from others with confidence.*
  Pope Leo XIII: Graves de Communi, *1901*

THE AGENT

Over the past decade selling real estate has become an attractive occupation to many people. They've been enticed toward it by talk of making lots of money, on one's own time, with virtually no education or even talent required. "What's to lose? I'll try it."

This has resulted in a witticism among 20 percent of the real-estate agents that the other 80 percent of today's agents are not seriously minded about a real-estate career (and that's no joke). They may leisurely come and go—sometimes a fireman, sometimes an engineer, sometimes a housewife, sometimes an insurance salesman, sometimes enjoying retirement—and sometimes sell real estate. These temporary agents fade in and out of the profession so often they are hardly noticed—except by an unknowing client.

But what about the full-time 20 percent of the real-estate-agent population? Are they professionals? They are; and selling real estate professionally entails a great deal of time, specialized knowledge, adept salesmanship, communication skills, legal know-how, and awareness of aesthetics. It is their talent that is invaluable during the negotiations between buyer and seller.

So it is only fair that these professionals make a good living selling real estate; and it is true that in some areas about 20 percent of the agents make about 80 percent of the money. Why this imbalance?

A major reason quality agents are in the minority is that one must fulfill only three qualifications to become an agent: be 18 years or older, pass a real-estate licensing exam, and pay a minimal license fee. That is it; and although the exam is difficult, there are no restrictions on retaking it if one fails.

What further promotes the lack of stability in this field is the way in which one can accumulate the knowledge to pass the exam. Courses that last two to five days are common, and one is free to take the test after personal study only. After passing the exam, the typical new agent tries to become affiliated with a real-estate office. (This is relatively easy because selling real estate is all commission work, and most offices are fairly anxious to have new agents expand their activities.) But wait. Before these new agents can actually begin selling homes, they have to wait about six weeks to receive their licenses in the mail. By then they probably couldn't remember enough to repass the exam if they had to. The odds are that such people won't last long as real-estate agents.

Fortunately, this route is not taken by all agents. There are aspiring real-estate agents, with professional career goals, who attend substantive training programs. They seek the experience it takes to become good at their profession. It will be to your advantage to have one of these agents working for you.

THE BROKER
There is a difference between a real-estate *agent* and a real-estate *broker*. An agent is self-employed (an independent

contractor) and works in an office operating under the license of a real-estate broker.

A broker often must have two years of real-estate experience as an agent in addition to several semester units of various related courses (for example, law, appraisal and finance). After a broker opens a real estate office (there must be at least one broker in an office), he or she may hire an unlimited number of agents. To a point, brokers are legally responsible for their agents' conduct since they act as supervisors over their agents' activities.

For every real-estate transaction that an agent completes, he or she receives a commission, which is usually split 50-50 with the broker. (The percentage split can vary, depending upon the office and the expertise of the agent.) The broker's portion is personal profit after office expenses are paid. However, a good broker will reinvest a major portion of that profit back into the business. (This could mean extras like a full-time secretary, or a computer hookup for quick reference to local listing activities, all for the purpose of giving better service to home buyers.)

NOTE: Specific qualifications for becoming an agent or a broker vary from state to state, though a model licensing law has been suggested. Some states also require agents to show proof they've put in a few hours in continuing-education courses every few years—a *small* regulatory effort to keep agents' skills current.

HOW TO FIND A GOOD AGENT

Choose a real-estate agent with care, just as you would choose any professional to work for you.

Make sure your agent works full time at his or her job. A full-time professional will be able to devote more time to you as a client. This agent will be able to offer the best selection of available homes based on your income, needs and preferences. Then, once you begin negotiating with the sellers, such an agent will be abreast of current market information concerning bank financing, interest rates and creative financing trends—and which of these options will be best for you.

Unfortunately, real-estate agents do not get paid *unless* a transaction is completed; often they work hard for nothing. Therefore, some agents occasionally may *not* mention a significant point in order to save a contract. For example, a young couple bought a three-bedroom, two-bath house, which involved a short-term second mortgage. After three years these buyers had to refinance the home to pay off that loan. But the appraiser for the new lender said that the home had only two bedrooms, not three.

The new homeowners were shocked! No one had told them (not even their own agent, who knew) that the back bedroom was an add-on—without building permits or the proper specifications to be called a bedroom. Their agent could have warned them that, as a two-bedroom house, a future appraisal would come in lower than that for a three-bedroom home. After three years there was not enough equity, based on that low appraisal, for this couple to qualify for a new loan. They lost their home to foreclosure.

You should search for a responsible agent who is completely knowledgeable, and professional enough to represent your best interests (even over his or her commission) on a full-time basis.

Choose an agent familiar with the area of your choice. Try to find an agent who works exclusively in the town or part of town you have decided to live in. Ask the agent questions such at these: What is the real-estate value of the neighborhood today? What is its future value expected to be? Are there special reasons why a home in this area might grow in equity faster than a home in another area? How are the schools, available shopping and public transportation? What are the local taxes, zoning ordinances and building codes? Are there any easements on the property?

Ask the agent what sources are available to him or her in searching for your new home. Your agent should at least subscribe to the local multiple-listing sheets and be knowledgeable about real-estate listings in the newspapers. (The real-estate classified section includes exclusive offers by other agents and for-sale-by-owner ads. Both of these sources often can be tapped by a good agent.)

Get a recommendation. In choosing an agent, personal recommendations are often your best leads. But even if your closest friend recommends an agent, check the agent's qualifications on the basis of the points just discussed.

If you are seeking to buy a home in an area unknown to you and have no one to recommend an agent to you, locate a reputable and active real-estate office by calling the local real estate board (listed in the phone book), or simply by asking around town.

Once you have located an office that sounds as if it might meet your needs, call the office manager, who is likely to be the agent with the most expertise. Managers also often carry an extra work load with their title, so if it seems that he or she won't be able to spend the amount of time with you that you desire, ask for the name and background of the next most qualified agent in the office. If you feel you simply are being referred to the next available agent, question him or her further, or go elsewhere.

Question a potential agent on creative financing. Real estate is a constantly changing industry. New applications of laws, regulations and entrepreneurial practices are continually being put to use. Make sure your agent has experience with the creative as well as conventional financing methods, or at least has a general knowledge of and the confidence to pursue creative financing techniques.

ence with the creative as well as conventional financing methods, or at least has a general knowledge of and the confidence to pursue creative financing techniques.

ESTABLISHING AN ETHICAL RELATIONSHIP WITH A REAL-ESTATE AGENT

Every realtor pledges himself or herself to a code of ethics which was originally established in 1913—though the code has been amended several times since. There are 24 articles in the code, which promotes high moral attitudes. Here are two of those articles:

ARTICLE TWO: In justice to those who place their interests in his care, the REALTOR should endeavor always to be informed regarding laws, proposed legislation, governmental regulations, public policies, and current market conditions in order to be in a position to advise his clients properly.

ARTICLE SEVEN: In accepting employment as an agent, the REALTOR pledges himself to protect and promote the interests of the client. This obligation of absolute fidelity to the client's interests is primary, but it does not relieve the REALTOR of the obligation to treat fairly all parties to the transaction.

These are examples of what you should expect from your realtor.

Agents can work with as many separate buyers and sellers at one time as they choose. When working with a seller, the seller and agent sign a contract, called a selling agreement, giving the agent selling rights to that home for a certain period of time, usually one to six months. In this contract, the seller also agrees to pay the agent a commission for his or her services; typically the commission is between 5 percent and 8 percent of the home's selling price. Here it should be emphasized that *although you may be led to believe these percentages are regulated and rigid, they are legally open to negotiation.*

This seller-agent contract can either be an "exclusive" or a "listing" contract. An "exclusive" means that no other agent can represent the seller *or* find a buyer to purchase the home during the period covered by the contract; the agent working under an exclusive contract represents both parties. This type of contract usually is written when a home is very marketable and/or is expected to be sold within a short period of time (possible it is a prestigious home or is very reasonably priced). An exclusive contract is financially beneficial to the agent because he or she will not have to split the commission with another agent, and it is beneficial to the sellers because they know that their interests are represented first.

A "listing" contract still gives the agent an exclusive right to sell the home, but *not* to find the buyers. The listing of a home that is for sale goes into the multiple-listing service of that area, and all agents, in all offices, receive notification that the home is being sold. At this point any agent can find a buyer, and when the home is sold, the two agents split the commission equally. (As mentioned earlier, once an agent receives his or her portion of the commission, it again is split with his or her broker.)

When a buyer and an agent work together there usually is no written contract between them, but a mutual understanding that the agent will try to find the buyer a home. Buyers always should work with their own agent! A buyer should not work with an agent who also represents the sellers, especially in today's market, when financing is the main concern. In cases where only one agent represents both parties, the agent's first loyalty is to the seller; after all, the seller is paying the commission.

AUTHORIZATION AND RIGHT TO SELL

NAME OF
OWNER _____ TYPE_____ DATE_____ 19___

For and in consideration of the services to be performed by _____
_____ , hereinafter called agent, I (we) hereby employ said agent
as my (our) sole and exclusive agent to sell that certain real property described below
situated in the County of _____ , State of _____ , to-wit:_____
_____

and I (we) hereby grant said agent the exclusive right to sell said property for the
price of _____
_____DOLLARS on terms of $ _____ cash; balance
payable_____
_____ and to accept a deposit thereon. This
employment and authority shall commence as of the date hereof, and shall terminate at
noon on the _____ , _____ , 19 _____ .   ["'NOTICE: The amount or rate of real
                (day)   (month)   (year)
estate commission is not fixed by law. They are set by each broker individually and
may be negotiable between the seller and broker.'']

I (we) agree to pay said agent _____
percent of the selling price or exchange value as and for compensation of said agent
hereunder in the event of a sale, exchange, transfer, conveyance, withdrawal, or
lease of said real property by said agent or any other, including myself (ourselves),
while this contract is in force or if sold within _____ days after such termination
to anyone with whom said agent had negotiations prior to said termination, unless
sold by another licensed real estate agent after said termination. I (we) further
agree that during the life of this Authorization to Sell to refer all prospective
buyers to said agent; not to negotiate personally with respect to a sale with
any person or persons who make direct inquiry of me (us); and, to cooperate in any
reasonable manner required to effect a sale of said property.

It is understood that said agent is a participant in the MULTIPLE LISTING SERVICE of
the _____ BOARD OF REALTORS, INC. and/or the _____ BOARD OF REALTORS, INC.
and that he shall submit this listing to be duplicated and distributed to all of the
participants of the MLS of both Boards. All these participants shall be considered
as sub-agents of the said agent and shall carry on all negotiations through him,
under the terms and conditions of this listing.

Evidence of good merchantable title to be in the form of Deed and Policy of Title
Insurance issued by a responsible title company. Seller agrees to pay____% (percent)
of the cost of the title insurance policy and escrow fees. Interest, taxes & rents
to be prorated. Insurance shall be prorated, or cancelled at the option of the
purchaser.

This agreement is made in triplicate and I acknowledge that I have read & understand
this agreement, and that I have received a copy hereof.

Dated_____ , 19___   _____

Owner_____   Address_____

Owner_____   City_____ State_____

Owner_____   Zip_____ Phone_____

In consideration of the above, Agent agrees to use diligence in procuring a purchaser.

Agent_____   Address_____

By_____   Phone_____

There has always been some discussion over who actually pays the agent's commission. Whether there are one or two agents involved, the commission is subtracted from the amount of cash equity received by the seller at the time the transaction is completed. However, many say the buyer pays because the commission was added onto the asking price of the home. Not so. The marketable value of any home does not drop even when an agency is not involved. A seller, selling on his or her own, will ask the same price as a person using an agent. The seller pays!

Following this train of thought—that the seller is paying all agency fees—it seems that even the agent who represents the buyer is supposed to think of the seller's interests first. Again this is not what happens. When an agent works with the buyer alone, the agent will work as hard as possible to represent the buyer fully during the search for the home and during the negotiations, in order not to lose that buyer as a client.

Still, because of the broadening spectrum of financing methods in use today, some buyers want to take an extra step to make sure they are completely represented. Thus, signing a "buyer's-broker agreement" is becoming established as a customary practice in some areas. This agreement is a written contract between agent and buyer for a set fee or for a commission percentage of the home's selling price. The buyers pay their agent, and the sellers pay theirs; both parties are exclusively represented. The sellers' agent's fee will be paid from equity when the home is sold. The buyers' agent's fee will be extra cash, in addition to the selling price of the home. This essentially means more money is advanced by the buyer at the time of closing for the home. In most situations a buyer's-broker agreement is unnecessary, but it is an option. If you decide, as a buyer, to use this method of contracting the services of an agent, then the selling price of the home *or* the percentage of the sale price that will be received as commission by the selling agent should be negotiated downward to reflect your having paid for your own representation. (If the home was listed, the seller's agency already was expecting to receive only half of the total contracted percentage anyway.)

LIFE WITHOUT AGENTS

There is one other route to take: buying completely on your own, or hiring an agent for advice only. If you are a buyer with the confidence to *do most* of the searching, negotiating and paperwork for yourself, a little professional advice may be all you will need. Find an agent, possibly a qualified friend, who simply will be on call for you for a minimal set fee. This fee may be as little as a good meal and a night out on the town.

It is completely legal and ethical for you to establish such a relationship with an agent. But remember, you are on your own to save money. So, to make your work worthwhile, make sure the price of the home you buy can be negotiated to at least three percent below its market value. (The seller can drop the selling price of the home, or the seller's agent can forgo a portion of his or her commission.) Doing the work of an agent on your own can bring on an occasional headache, so the outcome of negotiations should benefit you. If the seller and his or her agent won't offer you a price break on the home, then get your own agent to work for you—if the home is listed through an agency, it won't cost you a thing because, again, agent fees are paid from the seller's equity.

What you can expect from your agent has already been mentioned. There also is something your agent should expect from you: honesty. Some say that a buyer should engage as many agents as the buyer chooses, for surely one of these will find the home the buyer is looking for, and as soon as possible. This is unfair to the agents involved. An agent is paid strictly on commission and does a great deal of preliminary work to find you a home. The agent is not paid unless he or she finds the house that you buy. So, if you approach more than one agent, tell each of these agents that you have done this. You may not get the results you want as quickly—why should each agent be zealous in his or her home-hunting efforts for you with such a good chance that you will end up buying from one of the other agents—but at least you will not deceive agents into spending hours, even days, working for you with little possibility of getting paid for it.

You, the buyer, will be happier with the results if you find a good agent and let that agent know you'll be working with him or her alone. This gives the agent the security and ambition to expend his or her best efforts on your behalf. And the agent will!

CREATIVITY IN ACTION

In the late 1970s, Vincent and Leigh Lind bought their first home, in a rural area about 40 minutes from the major city where Vincent worked. It had been a very well-timed purchase, as more and more city dwellers decided that commuting to work was worth being able to live in this country atmosphere. The Linds' neighborhood developed a prestigious reputation, and after five years, the home's value had almost tripled!

After those five years, Vincent and Leigh spotted a larger custom-built, Cape Cod-type house under construction on a large piece of property not too far from their current home. Because Vincent's business had been very successful and because their family was growing, they decided to look into the purchase of this larger home.

The builder/owner was asking $325,000. Mr. and Mrs. Lind contacted a real-estate agent and friend, whom they wanted to *represent them; together they wrote up a purchase offer.*

The Linds offered to pay $290,000, of which $75,000 would be in cash; they would assume the builder's loan for $125,000; and the builder would carry a second loan of $90,000 for two years, with quarterly interest-only payments. Also, because another prospective buyer had already made an offer on the home—an offer that was contingent on the sale of another property they owned—the Linds did not include a contingency clause in their offer, and with it submitted a $7,000 deposit. (Buyers who submit an offer with a contingency based on the sale of another property usually have 48 to 72 hours to remove the contingency from their contract when a second, non-contingent offer, such as the Linds', is made. If the prospective buyers do not remove the contingent clause from their offer within that period of time, they lose their bid on the home.)

The builder/owner was interested in negotiating with the Linds, and made the following counteroffer: he would take no less than $300,000. This meant $10,000 more would be added to the second-mortgage loan that he would finance, and if the Linds wanted to work through an agent they would have to pay an additional 3 percent, in addition to the $300,000, for the agent's commission. (The builder/owner was also a real-estate broker and would not have any other agent involved if it meant he would receive less than $300,000 for the home.)

To save the 3 percent agent's fee ($9,000 in this case), the Linds decided to buy the home on their own; and their agent friend, who had been helping out so far, gracefully bowed out. The Linds accepted the builder's counteroffer with a final counteroffer of their own: for the extra $10,000 over the $290,000 they had originally offered, they wanted some general upgrading of the home in the final days of its construction. This included a fireplace in the master bedroom, a brick wall around the driveway, and tile and light fixtures in the bathrooms and kitchen.

Both counteroffers were accepted and signed. The contract became binding, with a 90-day close of escrow date.

The contract for purchase of the new home had been completed, but Vincent's headaches were just beginning. He had to take on all the chores of an agent by finding a title company, working with the banks, and making decisions—without professional advice on the many details that were to arise—all in his spare time!

Another major problem the Linds faced involved the home they already owned. The contract for the new home was not contingent on the sale of their present home, but if they did not sell that home, it would be difficult for them to advance the $75,000 cash they needed to purchase the new home. And Vincent knew that if he couldn't raise the $75,000, he would lose their $7,000 deposit.

The Linds put a for-sale-by-owner sign in front of their present home. The asking price was $255,000. They were worried about finding a buyer at that high price, particularly with the current high interest rates. Fortunately, their only offer was from a lawyer and his wife, who fell in love with the home and the neighborhood. For these buyers, the Bradleys, the only potential problem was their ability to advance enough cash to meet the Linds' needs.

The Bradleys offered $240,000 for the home; based on that price (and with no agents involved), the Linds and Bradleys sat down together to negotiate an acceptable contract. They chose a "subject-to" finance method, with a $50,000 down payment in cash; the Linds would carry a second mortgage for $9,000. The Linds also would refinance their current home loan (before the subject-to sale took effect) up to $181,000 which could then be assumed by the Bradleys, to get the remaining cash they needed. (That original loan also had been refinanced two years previously for extra cash to upgrade the house and to landscape; they currently owed $130,000.)

Remember, in a subject-to contract the buyers take title, but the sellers still are primarily responsible for the loan; in other words, in this case the savings and loan company was unaware that after *refinancing the home loan to $181,000, the home would change owners. The buyers (the Bradleys) simply would make payments to the sellers (the Linds), and they, in turn, would continue making payments to the savings and loan company.*

This contract was signed and, for the present, accepted by both parties. But a few days later the Bradleys verbally withdrew from their contract with the Linds for fear they could not meet its financial requirements . So the Bradleys and Linds arranged to meet again to renegotiate the contract, thereby making it easier on the buyers. (At this point, the Linds had little recourse but to save this contract if possible, since soon they would have to advance the down payment on their new home.)

Before the meeting, the Linds had their savings and loan company appraise their present home in order to refinance their current home loan up to $181,000. But the savings and loan company would refinance the loan for $170,000 only. Thus, the meeting became necessary for both parties to re-evaluate the situation.

Negotiations continued between the Bradleys and the Linds, and a new contract was written: The sale price remained at $240,000; the cash down payment would be $45,000; the Linds would carry a $25,000 second mortgage for three years with interest-only payments at 13 percent (the first six months of payments would be deferred), and the Bradleys would take over payments on the $170,000 refinanced loan at a 14 percent variable-interest rate. The contract remained a subject-to concerning the $170,000 loan, but with the agreement that the Bradleys would try to assume the loan as soon as escrow closed.

NOTE: Even though the refinanced loan was with a federally chartered savings and loan company (which normally does not allow assumptions), the company did, in fact, allow the Bradleys to assume the loan two weeks after escrow closed, with a minimal assumption fee of $100. This meant the Bradleys took over primary responsibility for the loan, and the subject-to relationship with the Linds no longer existed.

The many headaches of working without a professional agent continued to weigh on Vincent over the next few weeks. Making sure that all paperwork and financing arrangements were completed at the same time, and on two homes, was a major undertaking! Though he saved a total of $22,000 on both transactions by not working through agents, and even though he was an intelligent and successful businessman capable of handling the transactions, Mr. Lind said he would never do it on his own again—but he did do it this time!

Evaluating today's many creative financing approaches and discerning which is best for each buyer have added to the challenge and complexity of the real-estate agent's job. But as these and more creative financing methods gain widespread acceptance, real-estate professionals will have a greater opportunity to tailor loan packages to meet the needs of today's home buyers.

The next chapter discusses the complex paperwork and extra financial considerations involved in buying a home. As you read, you will develop a further appreciation of what takes place between the signing of the contract and the final day of escrow. You can consider further whether you have the confidence to buy your new home on your own, or prefer to have an agent working for you.

8

THE CONTRACT

Home is where the great are small,
and the small are great.
          Pope Leo XIII:
Graves de Communi,
                    1901

8
THE CONTRACT

For the past three weekends you have been looking for a home but so far have found nothing. Today is Saturday, and again you begin another day of wandering through houses and talking to the people selling them. But today will be different: You will find the home you have been looking for. When the decision is made to buy "that house"—no matter who you are, where you are buying or how much money you have—it is going to be scary!

The first step in buying a home is to make an "offer" to the sellers. Your agent (if you have one) will have the appropriate offer forms and will help you to complete them before approaching the sellers. If you do not have an agent, you should be able to find these forms at the local real-estate board office, at an escrow company, or at a real-estate attorney's office. Some of these offices will give you the forms *and* guide you through your offer to the sellers at your request (although most do not have the expertise of an agent). These offices do not advertise these services, however, because they like to keep strong relations with the real-estate agents who bring them most of their clients.

The offer form is called a purchase contract, which delineates all aspects of your offer; detailing such items as the financing to be obtained and even whether the drapes and refrigerator are to be included with the sale of the house. It should all be spelled out precisely. Anything structurally attached to the house, from a hanging dining light to an ornate fireplace mantle, ostensibly remains with the house, but it is best to discuss anything you have a question about, and then *write out* the decision in your contract.

It is customary for the buyer to submit a check, to be held as a deposit, at the same time the offer is presented to the seller. Usually the deposit is between $500 and 10 percent of the home's purchase price—each part of the country has traditions that will determine the approximate amount of your deposit. The deposit holds the property for the buyer until all negotiable points of the contract have been discussed and agreed to; this can take from one to 10 days, or more.

Negotiable points can cover a wide range: the seller thinks the offered price is too far under the asking price; the buyer wants a termite inspection completed, and then any subsequent work to be done and paid for before taking title to the home; the buyer wants the washer and dryer included in the sale; the buyer wants to split all escrow costs. When an offer involves these types of unanswered problems, the offered contract may nevertheless be accepted but *contingent upon* an agreement being reached on these particular points. Once the offer has been submitted by the buyer, the seller may present changes by attaching a *counter-offer*. For example, the seller agrees to the buyer's offer with the exception that the seller would like an additional $2,000 added to the sale price—the seller will sign the contract *contingent upon* the buyer signing a counter-offer form agreeing to pay the additional $2,000. Should something in the contracted offer be irreconcilable, the buyer will have the deposit check returned and then is no longer obligated to the seller in any way.

When the contract is completely agreed upon and signed by both the buyer and the seller, the buyer's deposit check is held (or deposited) until the day the property title changes name—that day is usually called the "closing day" of escrow. At that time the deposit is computed in the final financing as a credit to the buyer.

The buyer's deposit ensures the buyer's legal responsibility to the seller. If you, the buyer, are working through an agent, the agent can hold the deposit for you in his or her agency's trust account until an escrow account is opened, at which time the deposit amount will be transferred to the escrow company for holding. Or, depending on where in the country you are buying, the deposit may be held by the seller's attorney. If you are working without an agent, you unfortunately may have to entrust your deposit to the seller. ("Unfortunately" because if you do not complete the purchase of the home, the seller would have to be trusted to return the deposit money to you.)

Once the contract is signed by both parties, they are legally bound by its terms. Should either party break the purchase contract—this occasionally happens when one party has a change of heart (often called seller's- or buyer's-remorse)—the other party can sue for "specific performance." However, to avoid slow and crowded courts, the outcome to such a default will probably be the returning of the deposit monies to the buyer or the retention of the deposit monies by the sellers, depending on who is defaulting. But if the seller defaults it is more likely the case will go to court and be won by the buyer. This is because each piece of real estate is unique and the buyer has a right to claim that property if due to him or her under a legal contract. There is a special clause on some purchase contract forms that actually limits liability to the deposit monies (see point 12 of the purchase contract form opposite). You need not initial such a point if you want the other party's liability to extend beyond the amount of the deposit.

You should enter into a contractual agreement with a high degree of sincerity. But you may leave the contract unbinding for several days to "buy" more decision time by purposely adding contingency points. For example, you may sign the contract (1) contingent upon your qualifying for a specific loan, or (2) contingent upon your review of any damage found by an inspection for termites, or (3) contingent upon your receipt of an inspection report of the roof. Rejection of the contract because you disapprove of the outcome on one or all such points will allow you to continue house-hunting without further obligation on this contract. Keep in mind, however, that once you make an offer and advance a deposit check, the seller cannot legally accept any other offer for the home. So, though you may want extra thinking time, do not irresponsibly delay the seller in the sale of his or her home.

ESCROW

Escrow is an official clearing-house for the exchange of funds and the needed legal paperwork before change of title to a home can be completed. In the eastern United States, escrow is handled by specialized real-estate attorneys called closing attorneys. And in the West, it is handled by qualified escrow firms who perform basically the same activities, although methods may vary. Escrow activities can differ even from county to county, because transfer of property title always has been considered a local matter. Land use theoretically falls under state law; thus the federal government only controls financial guidelines for real-estate transactions. The American Escrow Association currently oversees escrow activities in the far

REAL ESTATE PURCHASE CONTRACT
AND RECEIPT FOR DEPOSIT

THIS IS MORE THAN A RECEIPT FOR MONEY. IT IS INTENDED TO BE A LEGALLY BINDING CONTRACT. READ IT CAREFULLY.

_____ . _____ , 19_____

Received from_____

herein called Buyer, the sum of _____ Dollars $_____

evidenced by cash ☐. cashier's check ☐. or _____ ☐. personal check ☐ payable to_____

_____ , to be held uncashed until acceptance of this offer, as deposit on account of purchase price of

_____ Dollars $_____

for the purchase of property, situated in _____ , County of_____ ,

described as follows: _____

1.   Buyer will deposit in escrow with _____ the balance of purchase price as follows:

_____
_____
_____
_____
_____
_____
_____
_____
_____
_____
_____
_____
_____
_____
_____
_____
_____
_____
_____
_____
_____
_____

Set forth above any terms and conditions of a factual nature applicable to this sale, such as financing, prior sale of other property, the matter of structural pest control inspection, repairs and personal property to be included in the sale.

2.   Deposit will ☐ will not ☐ be increased by $_____ to $ _____ within_____ days of acceptance of this offer.

3.   Buyer does ☐ does not ☐ intend to occupy subject property as his residence.

4.   The supplements initialed below are incorporated as part of this agreement.

Other

____ Structural Pest Control Certification Agreement   ____ Occupancy Agreement   ____ _____
____ Special Studies Zone Disclosure   ____ VA Amendment   ____ _____
____ Flood Insurance Disclosure   ____ FHA Amendment   ____ _____

5.   Buyer and Seller acknowledge receipt of a copy of this page, which constitutes Page 1 of ____ Pages.

X_____   X_____
BUYER   SELLER

X_____   X_____
BUYER   SELLER

A REAL ESTATE BROKER IS THE PERSON QUALIFIED TO ADVISE ON REAL ESTATE. IF YOU DESIRE LEGAL ADVICE CONSULT YOUR ATTORNEY.

REAL ESTATE PURCHASE CONTRACT AND RECEIPT FOR DEPOSIT
The following terms and conditions are hereby incorporated in and made a part of Purchaser's Offer

6.   Buyer and Seller shall deliver signed instructions to the escrow holder within _____ days from Seller's acceptance which shall provide for closing within _____ days from Seller's acceptance. Escrow fees to be paid as follows:

7.   Title is to be free of liens, encumbrances, easements, restrictions, rights and conditions of record or known to Seller, other than the following: (1) Current property taxes, (2) covenants, conditions, restrictions, and public utility easements of record, if any, provided the same do not adversely affect the continued use of the property for the purposes for which it is presently being used, unless reasonably disapproved by Buyer in writing within _____ days of receipt of a current preliminary title report furnished at _____ expense. and (3) _____

Seller shall furnish Buyer at _____ expense a standard Land Title Association policy issued by _____ Company, showing title vested in Buyer subject only to the above. If Seller (1) is unwilling or unable to eliminate any title matter disapproved by Buyer as above, Seller may terminate this agreement, or (2) fails to deliver title as above, Buyer may terminate this agreement; in either case, the deposit shall be returned to Buyer.

8.   Property taxes, premiums on insurance acceptable to Buyer, rents, interest, and _____ shall be pro-rated as of (a) the date of recordation of deed; or (b) _____

Any bond or assessment which is a lien shall be ___paid___ by _____ _____ shall pay cost of ___assumed___ transfer taxes, if any.

9.   Possession shall be delivered to Buyer (a) on close of escrow, or (b) not later than _____ days after close of escrow or (c) _____

10.   Unless otherwise designated in the escrow instructions of Buyer, title shall vest as follows: _____

(The manner of taking title may have significant legal and tax consequences. Therefore, give this matter serious consideration.)

11.   If Broker is a participant of a Board multiple listing service ("MLS"), the Broker is authorized to report the sale, its price, terms, and financing for the information, publication, dissemination, and use of the authorized Board members.

12.   **If Buyer fails to complete said purchase as herein provided by reason of any default of Buyer, Seller shall be released from his obligation to sell the property to Buyer and may proceed against Buyer upon any claim or remedy which he may have in law or equity; provided, however, that by placing their initials here Buyer: (   ) Seller: (   ) agree that Seller shall retain the deposit as his liquidated damages. If the described property is a dwelling with no more than four units, one of which the Buyer intends to occupy as his residence, Seller shall retain as liquidated damages the deposit actually paid, or an amount therefrom, not more than 3% of the purchase price and promptly return any excess to Buyer.**

13.   If the only controversy or claim between the parties arises out of or relates to the disposition of the Buyer's deposit, such controversy or claim shall at the election of the parties be decided by arbitration. Such arbitration shall be determined in accordance with the Rules of the American Arbitration Association, and judgment upon the award rendered by the Arbitrator(s) may be entered in any court having jurisdiction thereof. The provisions of Code of Civil Procedure Secition 1283.05 shall be applicable to such arbitration.

14.   In any action or proceeding arising out of this agreement, the prevailing party shall be entitled to reasonable attorney's fees and costs.

15.   Time is of the essence. All modifications or extensions shall be in writing signed by the parties.

16.   This constitutes an offer to purchase the described property. Unless acceptance is signed by Seller and the signed copy delivered to Buyer, in person or by mail to the address below, within _____ days, this offer shall be deemed revoked and the deposit shall be returned. Buyer acknowledges receipt of a copy hereof.

Real Estate Broker_____   Buyer _____

By_____   _____

Address_____   Address_____

Telephone _____   Telephone _____

ACCEPTANCE

The undersigned Seller accepts and agrees to sell the property on the above terms and conditions. Seller has employed _____ _____ as Broker(s) and agrees to pay for services the sum of _____ Dollars ($_____), payable as follows:

(a) On recordation of the deed or other evidence of title, or (b) if completion of sale is prevented by default of Seller, upon Seller's default or (c) if completion of sale is prevented by default of Buyer, only if and when Seller collects damages from Buyer, by suit or otherwise and then in an amount not less than one-half of the damages recovered, but not to exceed the above fee, after first deducting title and escrow expenses and the expenses of collection, if any. In any action between Broker and Seller arising out of this agreement, the prevailing party shall be entitled to reasonable attorney's fees and costs. The undersigned acknowledges receipt of a copy and authorizes Broker(s) to deliver a signed copy to Buyer.

Dated:_____Telephone_____   Seller_____

Address _____   Seller_____

Broker(s) agree to the foregoing. Broker_____ Broker_____

Dated: _____ By _____   Dated:_____By_____

COUNTER OFFER

THIS IS INTENDED TO BE A LEGALLY BINDING AGREEMENT — READ IT CAREFULLY

This is a counter offer to the Real Estate Purchase Contract and Receipt for Deposit dated _____, 19____.

in which _____

is referred to as buyer and _____

is referred to as seller.

Seller accepts all of the terms and conditions set forth in the above designated agreement with the following changes or amendments:

_____
_____
_____
_____
_____
_____
_____
_____
_____
_____
_____
_____

The seller reserves the right to continue to offer the herein described property for sale and accept any offer acceptable to him at anytime

prior to personal delivery to seller or _____, seller's authorized agent, of a copy of this counter-offer, duly

accepted and signed by buyer. Unless this counter offer is accepted in this manner on or before _____, 19____

at _____ a.m./p.m. it shall be deemed revoked and the deposit shall be returned to the buyer.

Receipt of a copy hereof is hereby acknowledged.

DATED: _____, 19____   _____
                                                                              SELLER

TIME: _____   _____
                                                                              SELLER

The undersigned buyer hereby accepts the above counter offer.

_____
_____
_____
_____

Receipt of a copy hereof is hereby acknowledged.

DATED: _____, 19____   _____
                                                                              BUYER

TIME: _____   _____
                                                                              BUYER

Receipt of buyer's acceptance is hereby acknowledged and seller agrees to sell on the terms and conditions set forth above

DATED: _____, 19____   _____
                                                                              SELLER

TIME: _____   _____
                                                                              SELLER

NO REPRESENTATION IS MADE AS TO THE LEGAL VALIDITY OF ANY PROVISION OR THE ADEQUACY OF ANY PROVISION IN ANY SPECIFIC TRANSACTION. A REAL ESTATE BROKER IS THE PERSON QUALIFIED TO ADVISE ON REAL ESTATE IF YOU DESIRE LEGAL ADVICE CONSULT YOUR ATTORNEY.

western states and hopes to be a national organization someday. It does not want to establish uniform rules for escrow, but would like to be a communications vehicle for dissemination of appropriate information on escrow procedures. Either through your agent or by personal investigation, become familiar with escrow practices in the area in which you are seeking to buy a home.

The amount of time a home is in escrow is specified in the contract. A home may stay in escrow for as little as seven days or as long as 90 days; however, escrow usually lasts from 30 to 45 days. The reasons for the specific length of time may vary: the buyer may need time to establish a loan, or to arrange moving details; the seller may need to move into a new home on a certain date; or (as is likely in the East) the lender may have a voice in the matter. If there is a conflict—for example, should the sellers not be ready to move until some date after escrow closes—the sellers can rent the property from the buyers for that period of time. Typically, the rent the sellers pay the buyers during this time is substantial as it usually covers all mortgage payments due on the property at that time.

One of the first activities that escrow involves is research into the title history of the property by a title company, which issues a title insurance policy, establishing whether there are any liens against the property—for example, outstanding mortgages, unpaid taxes, land conveyances for boundary rights, etc. It also includes facts about property assessments and property easements.

Because issuance of title insurance policies is standard in the western states, use of a real-estate attorney often is not necessary there. Where title insurance policies are not issued, an attorney's opinion is needed in every transaction. In most eastern states, even where closing attorneys are customarily used, it still is possible—and advisable— for the buyer to obtain a title insurance policy on his or her own.

Next, those handling escrow, or the closing attorney, will draw up all deed of trust notes (legally stating who will own the mortgage or mortgages on the home), a grant deed (which signifies the new owner), and an instruction sheet (which indicates the distribution of funds).

On the day escrow closes, you will receive and sign the instruction sheet; it clearly delineates the appropriate exchange of all monies that day. The following table lists expenses that might appear on your instruction sheet. You may be better prepared for these expenses by requesting an estimated statement prior to the day escrow closes.

Item	Approx. Cost
1. Conventional lender's statement fee (from bank or savings and loan company).	$15
2. Conventional lender's loan transfer fee. (This is an assumption fee and is supposed to be minimal. If you are charged more than $200—for example, you may be charged 1 percent of the home's price—the lender may unknowingly be breaking the law. Laws in this area are new and still changing, so look into the matter!)	$45-$200
3. Pest control report. (This is required only in some areas of the country. Payment for any work that subsequently needs to be done is negotiable; although tradition in your area may be the deciding factor.)	$75
4. Insurance: first year's premium. (Fire and possibly homeowners' insurance are required.)	$250-$500
5. Title company's insurance premium.	$150-$500

(This is based on the purchase price of the home. This estimate is half the cost, as buyer and seller can split the fee.)

6. Escrow fees. (These are based on the purchase price of the home. This estimate is half the cost, as buyer and seller can split the fees.) $75–$500

or

Closing attorney's fees. (Most often these are on an hourly basis, with a predetermined maximum.)   open

7. Official recording of deeds. (This fee is based on the number of pages.) $10–$15

8. Preparation of documents (preparation of notes; based on the number of pages). $20–$40

9. Down payment.   variable

Subtracted from these debits will be any credits that are due you as the buyer. The contract deposit always is a credit at the close of escrow, and this deposit may well cover all expenses listed above, not including the down payment. The following table lists possible credits (some may not apply in your purchase situation):

Item	*Approx. Cost*
1. Proration of property taxes.	The amount of all these credits will vary depending on the situation.
2. Outstanding mortgage-loan interest.	
3. Termite-work credit. (If it is agreed that any needed work will be completed by the buyers after they move into the home, it can be considered a credit on the instruction sheet.)	

4. Proration of assessments.

5. Proration of rent. (The sellers may rent the home from the buyers for a period of time.)

6. Deposit given to the sellers at the time of the buyers' offer.

On the day escrow closes, you will sign and receive copies of all paperwork. Then the keys to the house are yours! However, *before signing*, return to the home for a final "walk-through" to make sure the home is being turned over to you as you expected. (It is best to do this within the 24 hours before you sign the final papers.) You have a right to postpone the signing if conditions in or regarding the home are not as agreed in the contract.

THE EXTRA EXPENSES OF OWNING A HOME
If you have been renting, your monthly payments for housing will probably rise; otherwise life for you will go on as before—except that you will experience the pride and joys of owning your own home. And there are many: those who never thought of sewing will find themselves making new lace curtains for the bathroom windows; those who hated browsing will not be able to pass by a garage sale...

There are, however, a few additional expenses that can be unexpected to a first-time home buyer. Here's a list of some of them:

1. *Extra bills:* for water and for garbage removal (both commonly paid for by landlords when renting); also, telephone and utility bills most often increase after you buy your own home—so if you hadn't thought these bills were large enough to budget for in the past, do so now.

(About two weeks prior to your move, notify all these companies—water, garbage, phone, utilities—and make arrangements for transferring service. Sometimes there are delays or complications, so give everyone adequate notice.)

2. *Home maintenance items:* lawn mower, large trash cans, hoses, brooms, garden tools, bathroom plunger, fireplace screen, front-door mat, washer, dryer, etc.

3. *Repairs:* Any home, even one solidly constructed, will have occasional breakdowns. Something simple may develop, like a leaky faucet in the kitchen; so might a more major problem, such as rain dripping in through the garage roof. Be prepared—not discouraged.

4. *Taxes:* In most states, your home will be assessed for property taxes. Some states offer installment-payment plans. If it is more convenient for you, many conventional lenders will have your taxes figured into your monthly loan payments so that you will never need worry about "tax time."

5. *Insurance:* All mortgaged property is required to carry property insurance (fire and possibly homeowners' insurance). These insurance costs obviously will vary depending on the value of your home. Only the actual house structure is insured, not the land, so your insurance coverage will be based on an amount less than what you paid for the home. Your real-estate agent should be able to suggest insurance companies for you and obtain quotes from which you may choose.

CREATIVITY IN ACTION
Chandra Brian was in her twenties, a college graduate, and was working as a window display artist for a local department store.

Three years ago she inherited $12,000, and, at the time, she decided to invest the money by buying a home. She answered an advertising campaign for some newly constructed condominiums that offered a buy-down interest rate. This meant that when Chandra bought her condominium, the *builder* subsidized 3 percent of her bank loan's 13.5 percent interest rate for three years. This helped her qualify for a major loan by reflecting monthly payments of a 10.5 percent loan.

Ms. Brian's condominium cost her $75,000: she made a $10,000 down payment with her inheritance; she received a seven-year conventional bank loan for $50,000 (amortized over a 30-year period) with her buy-down interest rate of 10.5 percent for the first three years; and she financed a $15,000 second-mortgage loan from a private lender for interest-only payments at 11 percent.

Now, three years later, Chandra needed to pay off her $15,000 second mortgage and start making payments on her $50,000 loan at the higher 13.5 percent interest rate. Where was the money to come from?

Until now, she had been paying $457 monthly on the $50,000 loan and $137 monthly on the second-mortgage loan. Her monthly payments were about to increase to $572 on the $50,000 loan and the second-mortgage loan could easily increase to $215. In other words, her monthly payments could rise from $594 to a total of $787.

It was wonderful that she had built a large equity in her home; after three years these condominiums were selling for $105,000. But she didn't want to sell; and though it was possible to refinance for more money than she actually needed to help with the extra payments, she didn't want to do that either because eventually that extra money would be spent. Chandra's big problem was that current interest rates were much higher than when she bought the condominium; now, because of her income level, she was at a disadvantage in trying to qualify for a refinancing loan.

After talking with mortgage companies, private lenders and conventional lenders, Chandra found that there were two viable ways for her to refinance. One was to keep her first loan and simply refinance the second; the other was to refinance both the first- and the second-mortgage loans to give her one new first loan. In making her decision, Chandra had to consider (1) what her monthly payments would be; (2) the length of time of the new loan (she didn't want to have to refinance again in three to five years—although, if she kept her first loan, it would be due in four more years); and (3) if her new loan would be assumable by future buyers.

Chandra was amazed to find the variety of refinance packages available to her from the various lenders. There was everything from two-year, hard-money loans at 19 percent interest and with a 10-point finance fee, to 30-year government loans at 15 percent interest and with a two-point fee. But no matter which loan Chandra took it looked as if there were no way for her to avoid the higher monthly payments. (How "good" a loan she would have depended on where money was available, how much equity she had and her income and credit.)

Chandra finally took a loan from a mortgage banker who refinanced loans through the Federal Home Loan Mortgage Association (better known as Freddy Mac). They offered a 30-year loan at 15 percent interest, and with a two-point refinancing fee. This refinancing fee, for a new $65,000 loan, would be $1,300, and her monthly payments would increase to $850 a month. But Chandra would never again have to worry about refinancing, and this loan would be assumable by subsequent buyers if she decided to sell her home.

This was Chandra's decision, though she had other options. One of these options was to keep her first mortgage with payments of $572 a month, and refinance her second mortgage of $15,000. The best offer she found for a new second mortgage was at 15¾ percent interest, amortized over 10 years, with a balloon payment due in three years. There would have been a six-point

finance fee, and her total monthly payments (on both loans) would have come to $775 a month. Initially this looked less costly, as the points fee would have been only $900 (six points on $15,000), and the monthly payments would have been $30 less than refinancing the entire $65,000 into one new loan, as she decided to do. But in three years her refinancing worries and costs would have begun again. (Should the interest rates go down, Chandra has the option, at any time, to refinance at a lower rate, as there was no prepayment penalty on this new loan through Freddy Mac.)

A FINAL NOTE

It is important to reemphasize the necessity of buying a home responsibly, especially when you take on a short-term loan. When your short-term loan comes due, you will be at the mercy of the money market at that time. If money is "tight" (caused by high interest rates), refinancing can be difficult, both in terms of qualifying for the new loan, and in the new loan terms, which might well mean an increase in monthly payments. Plan ahead. Think positively about your future, and work to get what you want; you can do it. But because the future always is uncertain, don't scheme when you buy a home just to get in it. Don't select a home-financing plan just to solve today's problems. Learn what your choices are, and when you have found the best way for you to buy a home, buy it!

GLOSSARY

ACCELERATION CLAUSE: A term of a home-mortgage loan that gives the lender the right to call all sums owed immediately due upon a certain event, such as the sale of the home.

ACCEPTANCE: Favorable approval of an offer (purchase contract) by the seller. Acceptance of an offer means that both parties have signed a binding contract.

ADJUSTABLE-RATE MORTGAGE: A method of calculating interest payments by home-mortgage lenders, which was established for federally chartered savings and loan companies. ARM gives lenders virtually unlimited power to vary a loan's interest rate from month to month to keep pace with current market rates.

AGENT: An authorized representative acting in behalf of a client and working under the legal responsibility of a real-estate broker.

ALTERNATIVE LENDING COMPANY: A specialized home-finance company that often shares in the home's equity growth for a period of time after contributing funds to its purchase.

AMORTIZE/AMORTIZATION: Full amortization of a loan is the even distribution of loan payments (principal and interest) over a fixed period of time so that the loan is completely paid off at the end of the life of the loan. (A loan's payments can also be calculated by using a fully amortized loan-payment schedule, but with the balance of the loan due in a balloon payment in a shorter period of time.)

APPRAISAL: An official estimate or opinion of a home's worth as determined by a lender.

ASSESSED VALUE: A value placed on property for the sake of tax collection. (The assessed value can be the most recent purchase price of the home.)

ASSUMPTIONS: Taking over payments of and primary responsibility for an existing loan under all of its terms, without the loan's being renegotiated.

BALLOON PAYMENTS: Payment of a loan in one lump sum after a predetermined period of time in which smaller, regular payments have been made. Real-estate law states that any payment twice the size of the smallest payment is a balloon payment.

BREACH: The act of breaking a contract.

BROKER: A person legally responsible for the maintenance of a real-estate office and the activities of the real-estate agents working through that office, and who expects compensation for those activities.

BUY-DOWN: A creative financing method to decrease the interest rate for the first three to five years on a home-mortgage loan. The loan is subsidized by a secondary source (often a new home builder), thus allowing a new home buyer to qualify more easily for the loan.

BUYER'S MARKET: A market in which the buyer has better negotiating leverage than the seller.

CAPITAL GAINS TAX: A tax on the profit (equity) from the sale of property.

CLOSE OF ESCROW: Signing of final papers and exchange of funds for the sale of a home.

CLOSING COSTS: Costs for the buyer and the seller in addition to the selling price of the property. These costs are paid at the close of escrow.

COBUYING: The purchase by two or more buyers of the same property for the purpose of sharing the costs of homeownership by sharing the living space of that property. (This does not apply to a married couple.)

COMPARABLES: A recently sold home or a home for sale of about the same size, in the same neighborhood and in the same condition as the home to which a buyer is comparing it to determine whether the price reflects a fair-market price.

CONDOMINIUM: A unit within a multiple-unit dwelling; the owner of the unit has full title to the unit and has joint ownership in the common grounds of the complex with the owners of the other units.

CONTINGENCY: A point or condition of a contract that has not yet been accepted by both parties to the contract.

CONTRACT: A legal agreement between or among two or more parties that binds each to fulfill a specific promise or promises.

CONTRACT-FOR-SALE/LAND CONTRACT: A creative real-estate transaction method that allows a buyer to purchase property without qualifying for a loan.

CONVENTIONAL LOANS: A traditional mode of financing. (Commonly those loans which are acquired through banks, savings and loan companies, and government agencies.)

COUNTEROFFER: An offer proposed in response to an original offer that was not completely satisfactory to the party making the counteroffer.

CREATIVE FINANCING: An unconventional method of obtaining funds to purchase property.

CREDIT UNIONS: A cooperative association of members

(employees) of a company formed to save money, make loans and share profits.

DEED: A document that when legally executed, conveys title of ownership to a given piece of property.

DEED OF TRUST: A document that conveys title to property held in trust for one person (the owner) by another person who holds the home's mortgage (a lender).

DEPOSIT RECEIPT: A real-estate form used to acknowledge a money deposit from a buyer to bind an offer being made on a home (usually called a purchase contract/deposit receipt).

DOWN PAYMENT: A cash sum of money—exclusive of monies obtained from loans—used to purchase a home.

EASEMENT: The right, privilege or interest which one party has in the land of another owner.

ECONOMY: The system or management of the production, distribution, and consumption of wealth.

ENCUMBRANCE: Anything, such as mortgages, easements, or liens, that restricts title to a property.

EQUITY: The market value of property beyond amounts owing on mortgages and other encumbrances (in other words a homeowner's profit).

ESCROW: The procedure governing a real-estate contract transaction by a third party (by a lawyer or an escrow company, etc.) until the transaction is fully completed and title is delivered to the new owner. NOTE: In some areas of the country, particularly the East, escrow means an "impound account" and escrow, as the procedure, is simply termed "closing." Whenever the term "escrow" is used in this book, however, it is the procedure as first defined above.

EXCLUSIVE LISTING CONTRACT: A contract between the sellers of a home and their real-estate agent giving that agent exclusive rights to represent them *and* the buyers of the home.

EXISTING LOAN: A loan that is currently active.

FANNIE MAE: Federal National Mortgage Association. It is a private corporation and the country's largest home-mortgage lender.

FHA: The Federal Housing Administration. It is an agency of the federal government that administers insured loans.

FINANCES: The money resources of any party.

FIXED-INTEREST RATES: Loan interest rates that will not change during the life of the loan.

FORECLOSURE: Obtaining of title to and subsequent sale of property by a mortgage holder (lender) to pay the loan debt in case of default on that loan by the borrower.

FREDDIE MAC: Federal Home Loan Mortgage Association, the second-largest real-estate lender in the country.

GRADUATED PAYMENTS: Mortgage payments in which initial payments are less than they would be for a standard amortized loan but in which payments increase after five to seven years to levels slightly higher than they would have been for a standard amortized loan.

HARD MONEY: Cash borrowed under stringent payback terms such as high interest rates, an advance fee, and a short-term payback date.

IMPOUND ACCOUNT: A trust account that is established by a lender to accumulate monies to cover the cost of items such as taxes and insurance-policy premiums. The money usually is collected at the time regular payments are made for the loan.

INFLATION: A sudden fall in the value of material goods or services that results in a sudden rise in prices.

INSTALLMENT (SALES): A real-estate transaction wherein the seller carries the secondary financing on the home (becoming a lender to the buyer) and takes payments on that loan over a period of two or more tax years. Sometimes the term refers to a second (or third) mortgage.

INTEREST RATE: The percentage of the principal amount of a loan that is charged for the use of the money.

INVESTMENT: The advance of money with the expectation of profit therefrom.

JOINT TENANCY: The equal sharing by two or more parties as cobuyers in ownership of a property, each having full rights of survivorship (that is, if one dies, the other automatically becomes full owner of the property).

LAND CONTRACT: See CONTRACT-FOR-SALE.

LEASE/PURCHASE OPTION: A contract under the terms of which one party (the prospective seller) gives to another party (the prospective buyer) the possession and use of property for a fixed payment and a fixed time period; at the end of that time, the prospective buyer has the right to exercise an option to buy the property at a predetermined price.

LENDING INSTITUTIONS: A bank, or savings and loan company, that lends money.

LIENS: A claim on property as security for payment of a debt.

LISTING CONTRACT: A contract authorizing a real-estate agent (or broker) to sell a home on behalf of a seller.

MARKET VALUE: The amount of money a home can be expected to be sold for within a reasonable amount of time.

METHOD: A mode, process or way of doing something.

MORTGAGE: An instrument, recognized by law, that secures payment of a debt.

NEGOTIATION: A conferring, discussion or bargaining process to reach an agreement.

OFFER: The presentation of a contract for consideration.

OPEN HOUSE: Opening a home that is for sale for public inspection without appointment.

POINTS: One point is one percent of the principal amount of a loan. Points are paid to FHA and VA lenders to subsidize low interest rates, and are also paid to lenders as a service fee when refinancing a loan.

PREPAYMENT PENALTY: A clause in a loan contract that allows the lender to charge an interest penalty if the borrower pays the loan in full prior to the end of the loan's lifetime.

PRINCIPAL: The seller (as the agent's client); also, the base amount of money owed on a loan (the loan total minus the interest).

PROPERTY: Anything that can be owned; a specific piece of land, with or without a building structure.

QUALIFY: To meet the financial requirement of a lender when applying for a loan.

REALTOR: A qualified real-estate agent.

RECORDING: Making a record of a real-estate transaction by filing with a proper agency.

REFINANCE: Acquiring a new loan to pay in full a current loan that is due; also, to receive cash from the established equity in a home; and, also, to acquire a new loan at more favorable terms.

RENEGOTIABLE-RATE MORTGAGE (RRM): A method of paying interest on a home-loan package that involves short-term interest-rate renewals at predetermined intervals of a long-term loan.

RRM: See RENEGOTIABLE RATE MORTGAGE.

RURAL: A country or small-town living environment.

SALE-BY-OWNER: The sale of a home by the owner/seller without the services of a real-estate agent.

SAM: Shared Appreciation Mortgage, a special lender program that helps first-time homebuyers finance a home and later takes a share of the equity.

SECONDARY FINANCING/SECOND MORTGAGE: A loan that is obtained for the purchase of a home in addition to the first loan acquired for its purchase.

SELLING PRICE: The price a home actually is sold for.

SHORT-TERM LOAN: A loan that has a payback date usually two to seven years after the issuance of the loan.

SIMPLE INTEREST: A method of computing interest rates making interest due based on the unpaid balance of the principal at the end of each pay period.

SINGLE-FAMILY DWELLING: A single structure built to house one family.

SUB-ESCROW: A second, nonconcurrent escrow completed on a house in order to skirt lender rules that do not allow secondary financing.

SUBSIDIZED LOAN: A loan wherein interest rates are supplemented from a secondary source (as in buy-downs).

SUBURBAN: Neighborhoods surrounding city centers.

TAX SHELTER: A financial investment, such as the purchase of real estate, made in order to have deductible expenses to reduce one's income taxes.

TENANCY-IN-COMMON: The sharing by two or more parties (as cobuyers) in ownership of a property, without the right of survivorship (that is if one dies, the other does not assume full ownership of the property; each partner has the right to will his or her portion of the property to another party).

THIRD FINANCING/THIRD MORTGAGE: A loan that is obtained for the purchase of a home, in addition to the first and second loans acquired for its purchase.

TIGHT-MONEY MARKET: A time in which loan money is scarce; commonly this is due to inflation and high interest rates.

TIMESHARING: Property bought in blocks of time. Most commonly condominium units will be sold by the week; the buyer purchases only those weeks during which he or she intends to use the unit, thus becoming co-owner of a single unit with several other buyers. NOTE: When you buy a time-shared unit, be sure you receive a deed to the property, not just the "right to use" it.

TITLE: A document evidencing a person's ownership rights to a particular piece of property.

TITLE INSURANCE: Insurance obtained from a title company that will protect a home buyer against loss if his or her title to the property is imperfect (if liens against or valid claims to the property were not discovered before the close of escrow).

URBAN: A city center. Urban living is living within inner-city limits.

VA: Veterans Administration, a federal agency that administers and insures loans to veterans.

VALUE: The worth of a property at a given time.

WALK-THROUGH: A home buyer's final inspection of the property prior to the close of escrow.

WRAP-AROUNDS: A creative financing method wherein the sellers continue to make payments on their original bank loan and receive payments from the buyers for that loan and for the secondary financing that the sellers are carrying. (The two loans are "wrapped" together for one monthly payment by the buyer.)

INDEX